Everyman's Poetry

Everyman, I will go with thee,
and be thy guide

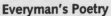

Thomas Gray

Selected and edited by ROBERT L. MACK
Vanderbilt University

EVERYMAN
J. M. Dent · London

Introduction and other critical apparatus © J. M. Dent 1996

J. M. Dent
Orion Publishing Group
Orion House
5 Upper St Martin's Lane
London WC2H 9EA

Typeset by Deltatype Ltd, Ellesmere Port, Cheshire
Printed in Great Britain by
The Guernsey Press Co. Ltd, Guernsey, C.I.

British Library Cataloguing-in-Publication
Data is available upon request.

ISBN 0 460 87805 0

Contents

Note on the Author and Editor

THOMAS GRAY (1716–71) is best remembered as the author of a single poem – the enormously popular *Elegy Written in a Country Churchyard*, first published in 1751. By the time of Gray's death just over twenty years later, the *Elegy* was already well on its way to becoming one of the most admired and imitated poems of all time. Yet Gray's achievement as a poet extended far beyond the frequently quoted sentiments of the *Elegy* to include the painful nostalgia of the 'Ode on a Distant Prospect of Eton College', the genial mock-heroic of the 'Ode on the Death of a Favourite Cat', and the complex self-parody of the 'Ode for Music', written in 1769 to celebrate the Installation of the Chancellor of Cambridge University. His ambitious Pindarics – *The Progress of Poesy* and *The Bard* – appeared to considerable critical acclaim in 1757. Gray's interest in the larger history and development of English poetry likewise led to his writing several experimental works in imitation of the Welsh and Norse poems which were then receiving enthusiastic attention in both academic and popular circles. Easily to be counted among the most learned and scholarly men of his age, Gray spent much of his life in Cambridge, first as a fellow of Peterhouse, and later (from 1756) as fellow of Pembroke College. He once wrote that he loved people most who, upon leaving this world, 'leave some traces of their journey behind them'; the works included in this volume present the essence of a poetic legacy the influence of which even Gray himself could not possibly have imagined.

ROBERT L. MACK is an Assistant Professor of English at Vanderbilt University. He has edited several eighteenth-century texts, including a single-volume edition of Horace Walpole's *The Castle of Otranto* and *Hieroglyphic Tales*. He is currently writing a biography of Thomas Gray.

Chronology of Gray's Life

Year	Age	Life
1716		Born 26 December in Cornhill, London. Only surviving child of Philip Gray, a scrivener, and his wife, Dorothy Gray (née Antrobus)

Chronology of his Times

Year	Literary Events	Historical Events
1716	Death of William Wycherley	Septennial Act passed by the Whigs extends the duration of Parliament to seven years 'Sinking Fund' established to reduce national debt
1717	Birth of David Garrick Alexander Pope, *Works* Thomas Parnell, *Homer's Battle of the Frogs and Mice*	Formation of the Triple Alliance between England, France and Holland
1718	Matthew Prior, *Poems on Several Occasions*	Quadruple Alliance (England, France, Holland and Austria) against Spain Society of Antiquaries formed
1719	Death of Joseph Addison Daniel Defoe, *Robinson Crusoe*	Occasional Conformity and Schism Acts repealed Westminster Hospital founded
1720	John Gay, *Poems on Several Occasions* Completion of Pope's translation of Homer's *Iliad* (from 1715)	The South Sea Bubble; financial chaos as investors are ruined by speculation in the stock of the South Sea Company Haymarket Theatre opens Peace with Spain
1721	Birth of William Collins	Robert Walpole becomes first or 'Prime' Minister (to 1742)
1722	Defoe, *Moll Flanders* and *A Journal of the Plague Year*	Atterbury Plot; High Churchman Francis Atterbury is exiled for contact with the Pretender (James Edward Stuart) An Act of Parliament (Knatchbull's Act) encourages the construction of workhouses for the poor

Year	Age	Life
1725	8	Sent to Eton College; under the care of his uncle Robert Antrobus, an assistant Master at the school. Meets and becomes close friends with Horace Walpole (b. 1717), Richard West (b. 1716) and Thomas Ashton (b. 1716). The four together refer to their friendship as the Quadruple Alliance

Year	Literary Events	Historical Events
1723	Death of Susanna Freeman (Mrs Centlivre)	The exiled Henry St John, Viscount Bolingbroke, is pardoned and returns to England
1724	Defoe, *Roxana*	
1725	Pope's translation of Homer's *Odyssey* (to 1726)	Death of Peter I (the Great) of Russia
1726	Jonathan Swift, *Gulliver's Travels* and *Cadenus and Vanessa* John Dryer, *Grongar Hill* James Thomson, *Winter*	
1727	Gay, *Fables*	Death of George I; accession of George II Death of Sir Isaac Newton General Election
1728	Gay, *The Beggar's Opera* Pope, *The Dunciad* (first version)	
1729	Death of William Congreve Pope, *The Dunciad Variorum*	Methodist Society formed at Oxford by John and Charles Wesley
1730	Birth of Oliver Goldsmith Colley Cibber made Poet Laureate James Thomson completes *The Seasons* Steven Duck, *Poems on Several Occasions*	Walpole/Townshend split
1731	Birth of William Cowper	

Year	*Age*	*Life*
1734	18	Entered as a pensioner at Peterhouse, Cambridge (4 July); admitted 9 October. Walpole will join Gray at Cambridge – a student at King's College – in 1735. First extent poem in English ('Lines Spoken by John Dennis at the Devil Tavern') included in a letter to Walpole. Meets Thomas Wharton, a pensioner at Pembroke Hall
1735	19	Admitted (22 November) to the Inner Temple
1736	20	Left property by his aunt, Sarah Gray. *Hymneal* celebrating the marriage of the Prince of Wales published in the Cambridge *Gratulatio*
1737	21	Writes Tripos Verses (the Latin verses printed with the list of Cambridge Tripos candidates each year) *Luna habitabilis*
1738	22	Leaves Cambridge (September) for London, without having taken a degree; plans to pursue a legal career
1739	23	Embarks with Walpole (29 March) on a two-year Grand Tour of France and Italy. The tour will include stays in Paris, Rheims, Geneva, Florence, and Rome
1740	24	Begins writing *De Principiis Cogitandi* in Florence

Year	Literary Events	Historical Events
	Death of Daniel Defoe	
	Pope, *An Epistle to . . . Burlington*	
	George Lillo, *The London Merchant*	
	First issue of *The Gentleman's Magazine*	
1732	Death of John Gay	Colony of Georgia founded
	Richard Bentley's edition of John Milton's *Paradise Lost*	Academy of Ancient Music founded
1733	Pope, *Imitations of Horace* (to 1738)	Excise Crisis; Walpole abandons scheme to reorganize the customs and impose a heavy Excise Tax
1734	Pope, *An Essay on Man*	General Election
		University of Gottingen founded by George II
1735	Pope, *An Epistle to Arbuthnot*	
	Henry Brooke, *The Fool of Quality*	
1736		Porteous Riots in Edinburgh
1737	James and Charles Wesley, *Psalms and Hymns*	Death of Queen Caroline
1738	Samuel Johnson, *London*	
1739	Henry Fielding, *The Champion* (to 1741)	War (the 'War of Jenkins' Ear') declared against Spain
	Swift, *Verses on the Death of Doctor Swift*	
1740	Cibber, *An Apology for*	War of the Austrian Succession

Year	Age	Life
1741	25	Quarrels with Walpole and returns alone to England, via Milan, Lyon, and Paris. Death of Philip Gray (6 November)
1742	26	Plans to study law in London with Richard West. Visits his uncle Jonathan Rogers at Stoke Poges in Buckinghamshire (May–October), returning only briefly to London in mid-summer. Writes the 'Ode on the Spring' which he sends to West, not knowing that his friend had already died (1 June). Writes the 'Sonnet on the Death of Richard West' and the 'Ode to Adversity'; perhaps begins writing the *Elegy*. Returns to Cambridge (15 October) as fellow-commoner and writes the 'Hymn to Ignorance'. Uncle Jonathan Rogers dies (21 October) and Gray's mother leaves Cornhill to live with her sister at West End House at Stoke Poges
1743	27	Granted a Bachelor of Laws degree
1745	29	Reconciled with Walpole
1746	30	Shares some of his poetry with Walpole, who has begun living in an apartment within the precincts of Windsor Castle

Year	Literary Events	Historical Events
	the Life of Colley-Cibber David Hume, *A Treatise of Human Nature* Samuel Richardson, *Pamela* (to 1741)	
1741		General Election
1742	Pope, *The New Dunciad* William Collins, *Persian Eclogues* Fielding, *Joseph Andrews* Edward Young, *The Complaint, or, Night Thoughts* (to 1745)	Walpole resigns and is created Earl of Orford
1743	Fielding, *Jonathan Wild* Robert Blair, *The Grave*	Battle of Dettingen
1744	Death of Alexander Pope Mark Akenside, *The Pleasure of Imagination* Joseph Warton, *The Enthusiast* Johnson, *Life of Mr Richard Savage*	Ministry of Henry Pelham
1745	Death of Swift	Jacobite Rebellion; the forces of Charles Edward, the Young Pretender ('Bonnie Prince Charlie') invade Scotland and are eventually defeated at the Battle of Culloden (1746)
1746	William Collins, *Odes on Several Descriptive and*	

Year	Age	Life
1747	31	Writes 'Ode on the Death of a Favourite Cat' at Walpole's request. The *Ode on a Distant Prospect of Eton College* (the *Eton Ode*) published (May) by Robert Dodsley. Walpole leases Strawberry Hill in Twickenham, which he begins turning into a gothic 'castle'
1748	32	The 'Ode on Spring' and 'Ode on the Death of a Favourite Cat' published (January) in Dodsley's *Collection of Poems*. Meets and befriends William Mason, who will become a fellow of Pembroke College in 1749 and eventually serve as Gray's literary executor. Childhood home in Cornhill destroyed by fire (March). Begins writing *The Alliance of Education and Government*
1749	33	Death of Gray's aunt, Mary Antrobus (November)
1750	34	*Elegy Written in a Country Churchyard* completed (June) and sent to Walpole, who allows the manuscript to be circulated among his friends and acquaintances. Writes *A Long Story* for Lady Cobham, a neighbour then living at the Manor House in Stoke Poges. Meets Henrietta Jane Speed
1751	35	The *Elegy* published in an authorized version (15 February) by Dodsley: an unauthorized version – the first of many – appears almost simultaneously in *The Magazine of Magazines*
1752	36	Plans to collaborate with William Mason on a history of English Poetry: begins *The Progress of Poesy*

Year	Literary Events	Historical Events
	Allegorical Subjects Joseph Warton, *Odes on Various Subjects*	
1747	Thomas Wharton, *The Pleasures of Melancholy* Samuel Richardson's *Clarissa* (to 1748)	General Election
1748	*A Collection of Poems by Several Hands*, edited by Robert Dodsley James Thomson, *The Castle of Indolence* Tobias Smollett, *Gil Blas* and *Roderick Random* Hume, *Philosophical Essays Concerning Human Understanding*	Peace of Aix-la-Chappelle (with France) ends the War of the Austrian Succession
1749	Fielding, *Tom Jones* Johnson, *The Vanity of Human Wishes* William Collins, *Ode on the Popular Superstitions of the Highlands of Scotland*	
1750	Johnson begins *The Rambler* (to 1752)	
1751	Birth of Richard Brinsley Sheridan Fielding, *Amelia* Smollett, *Peregrine Pickle*	Death of Frederick, Prince of Wales; succeeded as heir by his twelve-year-old son, George Gin Act curbs excessive drinking
1752	Christopher Smart, *Poems on Several Occasions*	Gregorian Calender adopted

Year	Age	Life
1753	37	Death of Dorothy Gray (11 March) at Stoke Poges. Dodsley publishes *Designs by Mr. R. Bentley for Six Poems by Mr. T. Gray* (29 March)
1754	38	Completes *The Progress of Poesy*
1755	39	Declines offer to become Secretary to the Earl of Bristol, in Lisbon
1756	40	Forsakes Peterhouse for Pembroke College, following an undergraduate prank
1757	41	Declines the Poet Laureateship offered to him following the death of Colley Cibber. Completes *The Bard*, which is published along with *The Progress of Poesy* in the volume *Odes by Mr Gray*, printed by Walpole at his new Strawberry Hill press
1758	42	Death of his aunt Mrs Jonathan Rogers (1 September) precipitates the severing of Gray's connection with Stoke Poges
1759	43	Moves to apartments in Southampton Row, London, in July, in order to study at the newly opened British Museum
1760	44	Visits Henrietta Jane Speed at the home of her friend Mrs Jennings at Shiplake, in Oxfordshire

Year	Literary Events	Historical Events
	Birth of Frances Burney Charlotte Lennox, *The Female Quixote*	
1753	Smollett, *Ferdinand, Count Fathom* Richardson, *Sir Charles Grandison* (to 1754)	French drive the English from the Ohio Valley and found Fort Duquesne (Pittsburgh) Jewish Naturalization Bill (repealed 1754)
1754	Death of Henry Fielding	Ministry of the Duke of Newcastle
1755	Johnson, *Dictionary of the English Language* Fielding, *Journal of a Voyage to Lisbon*	
1756	Birth of William Godwin	Beginning of the Seven Years' War against France; Alliance of Britain and Prussia against France, Austria and Russia; William Pitt, as Minister in charge of War, prosecutes the conflict with vigour Black Hole of Calcutta
1757	Edmund Burke, *A Philosophical Enquiry into the Origin of our Ideas of the Sublime and the Beautiful* John Dyer, *The Fleece* Birth of William Blake	Victory of Clive at the Battle of Plassey (India); British hegemony in the subcontinent established
1758	Johnson, *The Idler* (to 1760)	
1759	Johnson, *Rasselas* Death of William Collins Birth of Robert Burns	Capture of Quebec by General Wolfe; capture of Fort Duquesne by the English British Museum opens Wedgwood Potteries founded
1760	Sterne, *Tristram Shandy* (to 1767) James Macpherson, *Fragments of Ancient Poetry Collected in the*	

Year	Age	Life
1761	45	Writes 'The Fatal Sisters' and 'The Descent of Odin', both of which are partly inspired by James Macpherson's recent 'Ossian' poems, and by his own research into early Welsh and Icelandic poetry. Writes 'Song' ('Midst beauty and pleasure's gay triumphs to languish') for Miss Speed. Leaves London and returns to Cambridge (November)
1762	46	Meets Norton Nicholls, a Cambridge undergraduate, who becomes a close friend. Visits Mason in York and Wharton in Durham (July–November)
1764	48	Writes 'The Candidate'
1765	49	Visits York, Durham, and the Scottish Highlands (May–October)
1766	50	Visits Kent (May–July)
1767	51	Visits York, Durham, and the Lake District (June–November)

Year	Literary Events	Historical Events
	Highlands of Scotland	
	Smollett, *Sir Launcelot Greaves* (to 1762)	
	Birth of William Beckford	
1761	Death of Samuel Richardson	General Election; Pitt resigns
1762	James Macpherson, *Fingal, an Ancient Epic Poem*	Lord Bute becomes Prime Minister
	Mary Collier, *Poem on Several Occasions*	
1763	Christopher Smart, *A Song to David*	Peace of Paris; Canada and India ceded to Great Britain
1764	Goldsmith, *The Traveller*	James Hargreaves invents the spinning jenny
	Horace Walpole, *The Castle of Otranto*	
1765	Death of Edward Young	Lord Rockingham becomes Prime Minister
	Smart, *A Translation of the Psalms of David*	American Stamp Act passed to finance the Seven Years' War (repealed 1766)
		Sir William Blackstone publishes his *Commentaries on the Laws of England* (to 1769)
1766	Goldsmith, *The Vicar of Wakefield*	Ministry of the Earl of Chatham (William Pitt)
	Smollett, *Travels Through France and Italy*	Death of James Edward Stuart (the Old Pretender)
	Thomas Percy, *Reliques of English Poetry*	Henry Cavendish discovers hydrogen
1767	Birth of Maria Edgeworth	Revenue Bill (taxing tea, glass etc.) enacted in the American colonies

Year	Age	Life
1768	52	Collected *Poems* published by Dodsley in London, and by Robert and Andrew Foulis in Glasgow. Writes 'On Lord Holland's Seat near Margate, Kent'. Appointed Regius Professor of Modern History at Cambridge
1769	53	Completes the *Ode for Music* (April) which is performed at the July Installation of the Duke of Grafton as Chancellor of the University. Travels to York, Old Park, and the Lake District (July–October). Meets and befriends Charles-Victor Bonstetten, a young Swiss student visiting London. Bonstetten is invited to Cambridge (December), where he stays in lodgings near Pembroke College
1770	54	Bonstetten leaves England (March). Gray tours the West Country with Norton Nicholls
1771	55	Dies on 30 July at Cambridge after a short illness

1768	Death of Laurence Sterne and publication of *A Sentimental Journey Through France and Italy* First edition of the *Encyclopedia Brittanica* (to 1771)	The Duke of Grafton becomes Prime Minister Russo-Turkish wars (to 1792) Royal Academy founded
1769	David Garrick's Shakespeare Jubilee in Stratford-upon-Avon	John Wilkes expelled from the House of Commons amid great public agitation James Cook's first voyage around the world (to 1770) Richard Arkwright's water-powered spinning frame patented James Watts patents the steam engine Royal Crescent completed at Bath Birth of Napoleon Bonaparte
1770	Birth of William Wordsworth Death of Thomas Chatterton Goldsmith, *The Deserted Village*	Lord North becomes Prime Minister (to 1782) Tea Duty instituted in American colonies Boston Massacre
1771	Birth of Walter Scott Henry Mackenzie, *The Man of Feeling* Death of Smollett and publication of *The Expedition of Humphrey Clinker*	
1772	Birth of Samuel Taylor Coleridge	Slavery declared untenable on English soil Second voyage of Captain Cook (to 1775) Kew Gardens founded

Year	Age	Life
1775		Publication of William Mason's *The Poems of Mr Gray, to which are prefixed Memoirs of His Life and Writings*

1773	Goldsmith, *She Stoops to Conquer*	Boston Tea Party protests the Tea Tax
		London Stock Exchange founded
1774	Death of Goldsmith	General Election
	Lord Chesterfield, *Letters*	Coercive Acts passed in response to the Boston Tea Party
		First Continental Congress meets in Philadelphia
		Joseph Priestley isolates oxygen
1775	Johnson, *Journey to Western Scotland*	Battles of Lexington, Concord and Bunker Hill; War of American Independence (to 1783)
	Birth of Jane Austen	

Introduction

By eight o'clock the light was failing. The loud-speakers in the tower
of the Stroke Poges Club House began, in a more than human tenor,
to announce the closing of the courses. Lenina and Henry abandoned
their game and walked back towards the Club. From the grounds of
the Internal and External Secretion Trust came the lowing of those
thousands of cattle which provided, with their hormones and their
milk, the raw materials for the great factory at Farnham Royal.

An incessant buzzing of helicopters filled the twilight. Every two
and a half minutes a bell and the screech of whistles announced the
departure of one of the light monorail trains which carried the lower
caste golfers back from their separate course to the metropolis.

Aldous Huxley, *Brave New World*

When Aldous Huxley's dystopian vision of the future was first
published in 1932, few readers in Britain would have failed to
recognise this passage which opens the novel's fifth chapter for
what it is – a deft parody of the beginning of Thomas Gray's most
famous work, the *Elegy Written in a Country Churchyard*. English
schoolchildren had for generations grown up reading 'The Elegy',
as it was more commonly known; many had at an early age been
set the task of memorising and reciting the entire poem, and the
rhythm of Gray's verse stanzas was unfortunately for some
inseparably tied to the switch of the pointer or the birch rod. Thanks
in no small part to the simple fact that the *Elegy* had been lisped by
countless young mouths in innumerable schoolrooms throughout
the country, individual phrases from the poem became a part of the
very language itself. The 'paths of glory' which 'lead but to the
grave', the 'storied urn' which memorialises the dead, the desert
flower 'born to blush unseen', the 'destinies obscure' of those living
and labouring 'far from the madding crowd's ignoble strife': Gray's
words and images lingered familiarly in the memory and could
often prompt the half smile of recognition or even, later in life, the
nod of sage and melancholy agreement.

Yet however much the *Elegy* was said to be cherished for the aphoristic brilliance of its language, it was valued even more highly for the supposed universality of its larger themes – for its success in impeccably articulating, as Samuel Johnson famously put it, time-honoured sentiments 'to which every bosom returns an echo'. Johnson's own biographer, James Boswell, was not alone when he looked to Gray's lines as a model for his own spiritual deportment in the face of adversity and, when overcome by the vagaries and seeming inequities of providence, stoically reminded himself in his own diary to buckle down and 'Be Gray'. And while Boswell would certainly not at first have recognised much of what was going on in *Brave New World*, he would in time surely have understood the relevance of a parodic *Elegy* in Huxley's grim vision of the future. Gray's original poem had, after all, exhorted its readers to reconcile themselves with their place, however humble, in the divine plan. 'Crimes' as well as virtues, the *Elegy* reminds us, are circumscribed by the necessary rituals of an obscure and uncelebrated village life; for every potential Milton who for lack of education had been left 'mute' and 'inglorious', the village graveyard might likewise hold a Cromwell 'guiltless of his country's blood'. Moreover, while we all may wish fondly to be remembered after our deaths, the quiet and grateful acceptance of our own modest destinies in this our temporal life is for each of us our primary task.

The opening lines of Gray's poem memorably place a lone observer in a rural churchyard at dusk. While the specifics of the setting remain deliberately obscure, Gray almost certainly used as his model the church and yard of St Giles at Stoke Poges in Buckinghamshire, where Gray's mother passed her later years and where the poet often visited her:

> The curfew tolls the knell of parting day,
>   The lowing herd winds slowly o'er the lea,
> The ploughman homeward plods his weary way,
>   And leaves the world to darkness and to me.
>
> Now fades the glimmering landscape on the sight,
>   And all the air a solemn stillness holds,
> Save where the beetle wheels his droning flight,
>   And drowsy tinklings lull the distant folds:

> Save that from yonder ivy-mantled tow'r,
> The moping owl does to the moon complain
> Of such as, wand'ring near her ancient bow'r,
> Molest her ancient solitary reign.

Companioned as he is only with these familiar bucolic sounds and with the lowering darkness of the rural twilight, Gray's narrator anticipates in his calm, almost serene observation of the world around him the tone of quiet resignation which motivates the *Elegy* as a whole. One of the paradoxes of Gray's poem lies in the acknowledgement that it is in such profoundly solitary and literally self-centred moments ('And leaves the world to darkness and to *me*') that individuals are allowed to recognise just what it is that binds and connects them to humanity as a whole. Hence the brilliance of Huxley's parody: in a futuristic world populated largely by 'Bokanovsky Groups' of Epsilon Minus Morons, where conformity is the dictated norm and in which individuality is looked upon as a grotesque aberration, poems such as the *Elegy* lose their meaning and need to be rewritten. In the very spot where Gray's observer once roamed solitary and alone, Huxley now posits high-speed monorails and people-movers filled with hundreds of 'lower-caste' workers. The sounds of a companionable nature have been replaced by the alienating blast of loud-speakers, the incessant buzzing of helicopters, and the screech of train whistles; the homely church steeple has been transformed into the crass and prohibitory communications tower of a Club House. The natural verdure of the lea has given way to the artificial landscaping of a complex of golf courses, and even the lowing herds of Gray's original have been absorbed into the vast assembly-line processes of mechanical progress. The scale of humanity has disappeared; individuality, in the brave new world of the future, has become a thing of the past.

Yet how many of today's readers would even recognise Huxley's parody? How many, for that matter, could immediately identify Gray's *Elegy* itself? Has our own world become brave enough and new enough so that poems such as the *Elegy* have indeed become irrelevant? We can only hope that the answer to this last question is no, and that the reasons for Gray's comparative decline in general popularity in recent years has been dictated by circumstances slightly more mundane (although anyone who has visited Stoke Poges recently may wish to disagree). That schoolchildren far too

young ever to appreciate the *memento mori* message of Gray's verse
are no longer forced to memorise it by rote is surely not a
circumstance to be lamented profoundly. The pedagogical virtues
of memorisation aside, the *Elegy* certainly benefits from being read
or re-read by a more mature audience, one for whom gravestones
and their epitaphs are themselves more than just the stuff of
Hallowe'en, or the morbid paraphernalia of some impossibly
distant future. Perhaps, too, the social and political conservatism
implicit in the *Elegy*'s message of quiet acceptance – its suggestion
that the poor and disenfranchised should silently and gratefully
count their blessings rather than stand up and challenge the *status
quo* – sounds too much like smug and condescending complacency
for some of today's readers. A generation which pretends to pride
itself on rectifying social injustice could hardly be expected to
endorse or to perpetuate the *Elegy*'s exhortation simply to resign
one's self to a divinely-ordained order which comprehends and
even sanctions the often brutal inequalities of this world.

Whatever the reasons one advances to account for the causes
underlying such shifts in literary taste and fashion, one is
nevertheless compelled to admit that the *Elegy* is no longer the ever-
fixèd literary mark it appeared to have been only a little over a
generation ago. Gray's poetry as a whole has slipped from the
nation's purview, and while it has not disappeared entirely, it no
longer enjoys the wide and comprehensive audience it once did.
That such is the case is unfortunate. Far from embodying an
anaemic timidity in the face of destiny or, alternatively, an out-
dated and stuffy conservatism in the face of social change, Gray's
verse has just as much to say to us today as it has always had. Apart
from the inescapable relevance (at least for the humanist reader) of
the *Elegy*'s own subject matter, the issues which on a more local
level motivate and enliven almost all of Gray's poetry – the tensions
between the public and the private, between what the poet says and
what he does *not* say, between what is articulated on the level of a
poem's imagery and what is kept suppressed or hidden beneath the
surface of a work – are as relevant today as they have ever been. In
an age obsessed with the transformative and alchemical potential
of an ever-expanding array of media, Gray's anxieties regarding the
act of poetic enunciation and the appropriative power of one's
audience are likewise concerns which are far from *passé*. We are
also, in other respects, in a position better and more fully to

understand Gray's poetry than ever before. The comparative licence permitted modern biographers can shed more light on Gray's personal life and the role of that life in the works; today's writers can ask questions which were quite frankly off-limits to an earlier generation of critics. We can thus take advantage of what is assuredly a temporary eclipse of Gray's general popularity not only to reassess and re-examine the place of the *Elegy* in what is now commonly referred to as the literary 'canon', but – ultimately – positively to re-evaluate the extent and the achievement of his entire poetic career.

Such a break with the past is thus in some ways a welcome one. Prior to our own generation Gray had for the most part been the victim of a surprisingly unimaginative critical consistency. To be sure, there had been a considerable amount of healthy critical attention directed towards Gray's work in the late eighteenth and early nineteenth centuries. Johnson's assessment of Gray's performance in the *Elegy* led eventually to a productive controversy regarding his larger achievement as a poet – a controversy in which Johnson's own judgements on Gray were more often than not harshly critical. Johnson in fact once described Gray's work as artificial and almost literally stilted: as a poet, he decided, Gray was 'tall' only by 'walking on tiptoe'. Wordsworth's genuinely problematic relation to Gray as a literary predecessor – his assertion that Gray did not write poetry in the language 'really used by men' and was more than any other author 'curiously elaborate' in his poetic diction – likewise fuelled critical debate. Later in the nineteenth century, writers such as Matthew Arnold and Leslie Stephen, both of whom devalued Gray's achievement as a poet, furthered the debate which often questioned Gray's niche in the literary tradition. Yet while one modern critic was no doubt correct in observing that 'since his time, there are few great names in English literature who have not left some . . . judgement [on Gray]', the substance of such judgements – since the late nineteenth century, at least – appears to have been more than usually consistent. The 'issues' which dominated Gray criticism in the early and mid-twentieth century (the dreary 'stonecutter controversy', for example) seem artificial and at times bizarrely contrived. Only very recently have we even begun to ask just why Gray's place in the established literary 'canon' remained for such a long time so readily accepted and so remarkably secure. Accounts of Gray's life and the relation of that life to his poetry likewise have had a way of remaining prudishly conservative and embarrassingly old-fashioned. Gray's poetic career is invariably presented and analysed as a series of erratic bursts of creative energy followed by long, fallow periods of pointless if painstaking scholarship or, worse still, simple convivial inactivity. While the narrative is for many a familiar one, it is probably worthwhile – before turning to the poetry itself – to take the time to recapitulate and gently to reinterpret some of the more important events in the poet's life.

Thomas Gray was born in Cornhill, London, on 26 December 1716. His father, Philip Gray, was a scrivener working in the City. His mother, *née* Dorothy Antrobus, maintained an 'Indian warehouse' or milliner's shop with the help of her sister Mary at the Cornhill address. Thomas was the fifth of twelve children born to the couple, and the only one to survive infancy.

A petition exploring the possibilities of a legal separation from her husband submitted years later by Dorothy Gray indicates that from the very beginning of their marriage in 1709, the couple had not been happy together. Philip Gray, who was probably an alcoholic, routinely abused his wife – punching and kicking her with such violence that she feared both for her own safety and for that of her small child. In an attempt to remove her son as much as possible from such a hostile and unhealthy home environment, in 1727 Dorothy Gray sent young Thomas to Eton College. There he could study under the watchful eye of his uncle, Robert Antrobus, who had already for some years served as an Assistant Master at the school. All of Gray's expenses were paid for by his mother; he was nine years old.

While at Eton, Gray formed several friendships which were profoundly to affect his entire life. A shy, retiring and unathletic youth himself, Gray found in the young characters of Horace Walpole, Richard West, and Thomas Ashton temperaments which naturally reflected and responded to his own. The four friends – bound together most by the fact that they all came from what would now be described as 'broken' homes and by their shared love of the literature of romantic adventure – formed an informal 'alliance' which set itself against the harsher realities of life at the college. To the eyes of Gray and his new-found companions, the meadows and fields surrounding Windsor were transformed into a veritable Arcadia; in their play they regularly acted out the classical narratives which they daily encountered and translated under the watchful eye of the schoolmaster in the classroom. All four young men moved through their early education at the expected pace, and the summer of 1734 saw Gray entered as a pensioner at Peterhouse, Cambridge. He was formally admitted to the college later that same year. Thomas Ashton had been admitted to King's College in August 1734; Walpole would join him there in 1735. Richard West, in some ways the most fragile and sensitive member of the now splintered 'Quadruple Alliance', was sent off forlornly to Christ Church, Oxford, alone.

The university town of Cambridge could seem sprawling and impersonal to new arrivals, and in his early months at Peterhouse Gray appears to have paid only half-hearted attention to his studies of history and modern languages. A lively and playful correspondence with Walpole – already sorely missed by Gray – at least resulted in some of the poet's earliest English verse and attempts at parody. When Walpole finally took up residence at King's in March, 1735, life at Cambridge became more bearable, and Gray settled down to work. His university career was distinguished if not spectacular, and he took time to write and publish several short poems in Latin, including a *Hymeneal* on the marriage of the Prince of Wales in 1736, and the Tripos verses *Luna Habitabilis* the following year. He made several new friendships which were to remain with him throughout his entire life; close companions now included Thomas Wharton, a pensioner at Pembroke Hall who would in time become a doctor, and the Revd James Brown, himself a Fellow of Pembroke.

Gray went down from Cambridge in 1738 without having taken a degree. He intended to practise law and had, in fact, been admitted to the Inner Temple as early as 1735. His aunt Sarah Gray, who died in 1736, had left him some modest property and income in her will; Gray was thus no longer entirely at the mercy of his parents' income. This financial freedom, such as it was, may explain why Gray seems to have had little qualms in delaying even the pretence of actually beginning his studies in the law. The possibilities of any serious career as a lawyer were in any event already growing slim when Gray received an invitation from Walpole to accompany him – at Walpole's own expense – on an extended 'Grand Tour' of the Continent. Such as offer could not reasonably have been refused by anyone, least of all by someone with a confessed passion for both French and Italian romances and for classical literature. The fact that the invitation came from Walpole himself, who was by then firmly entrenched as Gray's best-loved companion, ruled any pretence of reluctance out of the question; Gray was to accompany the son of the most powerful man in England on a tour of the Continent.

Walpole and Gray landed at Calais in March 1739. The early months of their tour found them caught up in the social whirlwind of the expatriate English community in Paris. They also made several sight-seeing tours just outside the French capital – twice visiting Versailles, for example – before settling on the comparatively small town of Rheims as a suitably placid and provincial place in which they could apply themselves with less distractions both to a study of the French language and to an understanding of the customs and habits of the French people. In time they travelled south towards Lyons and Geneva and, in November, endured a harrowing crossing of the Alps. The scope of Walpole's tour had been extended – with the permission of his father – to include several months in Italy, and Gray could now look forward to spending time on truly 'classic' soil. The pair soon fell into the hands of experienced cicerones in both Florence and Rome. Their letters home provide a fascinating, anecdote-filled account of life on the Continent in the early decades of the eighteenth century. Walpole's social status allowed him fully to relish the peculiarly Mediterranean gaiety and abandon of the social scene; Gray's more bookish temperament led him to more scholarly pursuits. At first the two were content to go their separate ways, but as the months drew on, the already pronounced differences in their personalities and respective interests widened and came to be a problem. In the spring of 1741 the friends quarrelled, and the resulting breach in their friendship prompted Gray to return to England on his own. While the exact nature of their dispute is not known, it seems likely that Gray's subordinate social and financial status, as well as the predictable stress contingent on their constant companionship, led the pair to grow, quite simply, short tempered and irritable; minor faults and shortcomings were magnified into great ones. Walpole followed Gray to England almost immediately, but the two would not speak to each other for nearly five years.

On his return to London Walpole could look forward to his new duties and responsibilities as an MP for Callington; thanks to his father he had been elected to Parliament while yet in Italy. Gray, on the other hand, was forced to create his own less pleasant diversions. The death of his father in November compelled him to look more carefully into the family finances and again to consider his own choices with regard to any possible career; the gap created in his emotional life by the abrupt severance of his love for and friendship with Walpole (the quarrel was tantamount to the break-up of a long-standing romantic attachment) was bridged partly by a newfound appreciation for the affections and talents of their shared friend Richard West. West – who was then living in London and who had grudgingly undertaken the study of law which Gray had himself so swiftly abandoned – was for Gray in many ways a better suited companion than Walpole in terms both of his interests and his temperament. Yet West was dangerously ill. At the same time that Gray was noticing the first signs of spring while visiting the home of his uncle Jonathan Rogers in Stoke Poges, Buckinghamshire, his friend lay dying of tuberculosis. West's tragic death may well have prompted the outpouring of poetry which flowed from Gray in the spring and early summer of 1742; the *Ode on a Distant Prospect of Eton College*, the 'Ode to Adversity', the 'Sonnet' on the death of Richard West and the beginnings of the *Elegy* itself all date from this period. The emphasis on loss, grief, affliction and nostalgia in each of these poems is perfectly understandable. Bereft of Walpole and now having lost West in earnest, Gray's life seemed truly to lack any sense of purpose or direction. He was desperately alone and deprived of two of the people who most gave meaning and purpose to his life. Having seen his mother safely settled into her new home of West End House in Stoke Poges, not far from her brother, Gray departed once again for the familiar surroundings of Cambridge, and for Peterhouse.

In December 1743 Gray took his degree of Bachelor of Civil Law. Although he at first attended lectures on Jurisprudence with some diligence, his time in Cambridge seems to have been spent primarily in slowly renewing old friendships and carefully cultivating new ones. He found the companionship of John Clerke, a Fellow at Peterhouse, and Dr Conyers Middleton, the University Librarian, particularly congenial. Sometime in 1745 Gray was, thanks in part to the efforts of an unidentified acquaintance, reconciled to Walpole, and not long afterwards he wrote one of his most light-hearted poems, the 'Ode on the Death of a Favourite Cat', in

memory of his friend's drowned pet cat, Selima. In 1778 this work
was published in Robert Dodsley's three-volume *Collection of Poems*,
along with both the 'Ode on the Spring' and the *Eton Ode*. In the
same year Gray's childhood home in Cornhill burnt down, and
shortly thereafter Mary Antrobus, one of his favourite aunts, died.
This latter event may have prompted Gray to return to the
unfinished elegiac poem he had begun some years before; a poem
which, though immediately informed by the deaths both of West
and of his aunt, in time metamorphosed into a meditation on and
lament for the inevitable fate (and the fundamental loneliness) of all
human beings. By 1750 Gray had put the finishing touches on his
final version of the *Elegy Written in a Country Churchyard* and had
sent a copy of the poem to Walpole, who instantly recognised the
achievement of the piece and enthusiastically encouraged its
circulation in manuscript. The poem was hurried into publication
by Dodsley in February 1751, by which time rumours had reached
Gray (correctly, as it turned out) that the piece was about to be
printed without his authorisation in a magazine he held to be
particularly disreputable.

The *Elegy* was of course an instant sensation, and in many ways
its success changed Gray's life forever. The comfortable anonymity
of his scholarly life at Cambridge was a thing of the past; much to
his consternation, Gray had become a public figure, and was
henceforth almost invariably referred to in a single breath as
'Thomas Gray, the author of the celebrated *Elegy in a Country
Churchyard*'. William Hazlitt was exaggerating when he wrote
years later that Gray 'probably died from nervous agitation at the
publicity into which his name had been forced by his learning,
taste, and genius', but that such an association and the fame (and
consequent exposure) surrounding it caused Gray no small amount
of embarrassment and discomfort can be surmised from the fact
that the only two significant poems which followed the *Elegy* (after
a space of several years) were far more densely allusive and
designedly more difficult than their celebrated predecessor. In *The
Progress of Poesy* and *The Bard*, published together by Walpole's
Strawberry Hill Press in 1757, Gray seems consciously to have
fashioned poems which, through their very style and choice of
subject matter, could have little appeal to an increasingly 'madding
crowd' of readers. If the two Pindaric odes, as they came to be
known, are indeed less accessible to the general reader than the

Elegy, in them Gray nevertheless pursued material which continued to fascinate him both as a poet and as a scholar; namely, the role of the Celtic tradition in British verse, and the broader history and traditions of English poetry in general. Gray's subsequent work – imitations of Norse and Welsh poetry such as 'The Fatal Sisters' and 'The Descent of Odin' – was to explore these topics of cultural, artistic, and national identity even further.

Apart from this general renown, and apart from having brought Gray to the attention of his aunt's more aristocratic neighbours at Stoke Poges (Lady Cobham and her relation, Henrietta Jane Speed, with whom Gray formed a close but by no means romantic attachment), the publication of the *Elegy* made surprisingly little change in the social pattern of Gray's daily life, if only because he refused to allow it to do so. He pursued his studies diligently, if slowly, and rarely strayed outside the familiar circle of his Cambridge acquaintances. Any attempts to draw him further into the activities of the social and political world seem to have been doomed to certain failure. (He not only declined the Poet Laureateship on the death of Colley Cibber in 1757, but had likewise refused an offer to become Secretary to the Earl of Bristol of Lisbon in 1755.) Aside from the limited and carefully executed imitations of Welsh and Norse poetry mentioned above, he wrote verse only occasionally and tended to limit the circulation of any such pieces to his closest friends. An undergratuate prank in 1756 prompted Gray to move from Peterhouse to Pembroke College where, thanks largely to the continued friendship of William Mason, he already felt very much at home.

Not all of Gray's time was spent in Cambridge, however. The opening of the British Museum in 1759 drew him for more than two years to London, where he rented lodgings in Southampton Row in Bloomsbury, and pursued his researches at the new facility. The death of his beloved mother in 1753 had severed any connection he had had with the rural retreat of Stoke Poges, but in place of the Buckinghamshire countryside Gray now travelled regularly to visit friends in Kent, Yorkshire, Durham and the Lake District. His journal of his tour of the Lake District, published posthumously in 1775, anticipates the fascination of the Romantic poets with 'sublime' landscapes of Cumberland and Westmoreland by almost twenty-five years. His correspondence to his many dear friends and acquaintances throughout this later period of his life remains to this day among the most learnedly allusive and elegantly crafted body of letters in the language.

By the time he had reached his late forties and early fifties, Gray had to some degree grown used to – if not entirely comfortable with – his status as England's most famous living poet. The collected edition of six of his poems which appeared in 1753 (accompanied by stunningly effective illustrations from the hand of his friend Richard Bentley) was the first authorised volume attributing the verse to Gray, and helped to secure his name; an enlarged *Poems by Mr Gray* published in 1768 established his reputation even further. While Gray himself scoffed at the notion that he could ever be 'tickled by the commendations of [other] people', he nevertheless took his position as the perceived heir to a great and venerable poetic tradition with becoming, if slightly baffled and humble, resignation. While the wide exposure of his work continued deeply to trouble him, the poet of the 'celebrated *Elegy*' himself took care always to maintain a dignity and decorum appropriate to his unsought and unlooked-for position.

As it so happened, Gray's last major piece of poetry was in many ways his most public and 'spectacular' one. In the summer of 1769 the Duke of Grafton was installed as Chancellor of Cambridge University in an elaborate ceremony at the Senate House. Gray was chosen to write the ode celebrating and commemorating the occasion. By this point in Gray's life comparisons to his earlier poetry and to the *Elegy* in particular were unavoidable. Gray to some extent took advantage of the inevitable, and constructed his own *Ode for Music* as a parody of and counterpoint to his most best-known work. The near-riot which disrupted Grafton's installation (the Minister was even then being pilloried in the public press by the vituperative and anonymous 'Junius') stole some of Gray's allusive poetic thunder, yet the rare achievement of the work remains undiluted. We see in Gray's last work one of the indisputably great poets in the English tradition knowingly and gracefully bidding goodbye to his craft.

If the 'Ode for Music' can be read as a kind of culmination of Gray's career as a poet – a sort of humorously retrospective and self-deprecating *vade mecum* to his poetry – his life was likewise to include one final, poignant and unintentionally nostalgic adventure of the heart. In December, 1769, Gray's friend Norton Nicholls introduced him to Charles-Victor de Bonstetten. Bonstetten, then twenty-four, was from Switzerland. He had spent the previous summer in Berkshire where, living with a clergyman and his family, he had pursued his study of the English language; he had met Nicholls while staying at Bath the following December. Gray was instantly charmed by the good-looking if slightly juvenile Bonstetten, and an invitation was soon extended for Bonstetten to join him for a stay in Cambridge. The invitation was accepted, and for three months the two read, studied, played music and worked together; Gray, some thirty years older than his guest, proudly and eagerly introduced Bonstetten to his aging circle of Cambridge friends and colleagues. Only after Bonstetten returned to Switzerland in March 1770, did Gray realise the true depth and extent of his feelings for the young man. 'I did not conceive till now', he wrote to Bonstetten, then in Paris, 'what it was to lose you, nor felt the solitude and insipidity of my own condition, before I possess'd the happiness of your friendship'. Bonstetten clearly savoured his conquest of the English *génie-poétique*, yet at the same time – to his credit – seems genuinely to have enjoyed Gray's love, kindness and affection. The two were never to meet again, but for a few months in the year before his death Gray once again at least glimpsed the 'sunshine of the breast' which had prompted his earliest work. Bonstetten, joining West and Walpole in what Gray had long ago affectionately called 'the first row of the front box of my little heart', completed the trilogy of individuals whom Gray loved as a man and who inspired him as a writer.

Gray's final months, which included an extended tour of the West Country with Norton Nicholls, were spent among friends and Cambridge colleagues. He died on 30 July 1771, following a short illness; he was buried at Stoke Poges in the family vault with his mother and his aunt. William Mason's edition of *The Poems of Mr Gray*, to which Mason prefixed an influential memoir of the poet's life, was published in 1775.

Most literary critics, when confronted with this narrative of Gray's life, have gone on to interpret his poetic career as a series of lost opportunities and tentative attempts to bring some sense of order to a troubled personal world. Like the three-volume Commonplace Book – crammed with notes in Gray's meticulous hand – which remains to this day in the Pembroke College Library, or like the similar notebooks in the Morgan Library in New York, Gray's story is itself read as the chronicle of an extensive lived only on the margins of experience. Even those critics sympathetic to Gray's achievement find themselves beginning to concede that the great poems were momentary lapses into what one is soon acknowledging to be an unearned and, in some ways, almost undeserved genius. More and more often, as the critical consensus shifts, we hear that Gray was not a great poet: he was a good poet – mediocre, even – who was fortunate on one occasion (and on one occasion only) to have genuinely caught the fancy of the public. Critics soon find that they are not discussing the merits of the poetry that Gray did in fact write, but rather that they are anatomising the problems of Gray's general 'artistic sterility'.

A mild alternative to such a sketch of Gray's career, should one at least wish to find more consistency in his poetic endeavours, is to suggest that Gray, at one with his generation in being denied access to certain types of lyric voice, fashioned a poetic career which circled uneasily around a 'sustained struggle to find certain decorous ways of talking about the self'. Such a view, while containing some small element of truth, shades all too easily into the teleologically deceptive characterisation of Gray as a 'proto-Romantic' poet. The reader is left with the Arnoldian vision of Gray as a poet who 'fell upon an age of prose'. Certain introductory volumes to the work of the Romantic poets which still enjoy a wide popularity among students and general readers alike have given an extended currency to this reading. The *Elegy* is singled out for praise, while poems such as *The Progress of Poesy* and *The Bard* are dismissed as 'abortive' or 'mistaken' attempts to establish a freer and wider use of poetic language. In other words, while Wordsworth eventually sign-posted the way towards the poetic high road, Gray's rural rambles led him only to a literary and linguistic *cul-de-sac*.

While selecting the poems to be presented in this anthology, however, it became clear to this reader, at least, that Gray's career as a poet depended to a much greater degree than has usually been acknowledged upon the responses of his audience to his work. More specifically, Gray reacted with increasing sensitivity to just what his audience *did* with his poetry once they read it. The course of Gray's career is admittedly difficult to trace in his own commentary on and reaction to the popular reception of his poetry. He affected to despise 'the Opinions of a Nation, where those who pretend to judge, don't judge at all: and the rest (the wiser Part) wait to catch the judgement of the world immediately above them, that is, Dick's Coffee-House, and the Rainbow'. Although he obviously cared deeply about the reception of his poetry, Gray was notoriously reticent regarding the popular reception of his works. The *Elegy*, for example, receives only a handful of references in his correspondence following its publication in 1751, only one of which – some commentary made in a letter to a friend in 1761 – would appear to judge the work to be worthy of any critical interest at all. Gray's reaction to the reception of the Pindaric Odes in 1757 is more fully documented in letters to friends such as James Brown and Thomas Wharton, among others, but that later correspondence seems already to have taken on the same tone of calculated, self-protective dismissal which Gray had by that time established in the poetry itself. To describe Gray's progress as a poet is to chronicle his persistent and at times almost desperate attempts to maintain authorial control over the interpretive activities of his readers. In emphasising these attempts I do not wish simple-mindedly to resurrect the view that the poet who found early fame and accessibility was disappointed when his later, more designedly esoteric efforts failed to find a similar popular audience. The focus of Gray's consistency is in fact a constant and determined movement away from the power of the critical audience and a sly, often mischievous reaffirmation of the power of the poet. Gray's attempts to maintain interpretive control over his works even as they were being published has of course been emphasised in studies of his later poetry. Yet the defence and possible reappropriation of poetic authority occurs not only in the Pindaric Odes, but in Gray's subsequent poetry as well. It is a move which, again, takes Gray into the realm of self-parody as the last, structural means of defence against (paradoxically) both misinterpretation and genuine understanding and comprehension. For Gray, parody and self-parody become apotropaic devices – means of warding off the malicious or simply uncomprehending horde of hacks, critics, newspaper parodists and common readers.

Of more significance is the fact that the inherent obliquity of Gray's verse only reflects the determined and intended obliquity of his life. The structures of parody came naturally to Gray, a man whose entire adult life (and whose childhood and adolescence as well) seem to have structured themselves around the ironic, parodic paradigms which signal the constant denial of any conspicuous essence. Gray enacted in his poetic career the parody which characterises his entire life. Indeed, Gray's life is a life lived *as* parody: from the earliest formations of a social clique at Eton which mirrored in its claims to exclusivity and power the kinds of treaties initiated by the government of Walpole's own father; through the adolescent correspondence which often amounts to nothing less than centos and pastiches of other writers; to, finally, a body of poetry which depends constantly on tactics of denial, deferral, reticence, restraint, ironic distance and references which point constantly *away* from the self.

It is worth emphasising, in the context of such parodic strategy, that Gray was a homosexual poet, and on some level demands to be examined as such. Gray's sexuality is the central, crucial and determining *fact* about his personal and poetic activity which has been clumsily evaded and implicitly denied by the host of critics who have analysed his poetry. Several critics have noted that the absence of Gray's obvious sexuality from discussion of his poetry has rendered any analysis of that poetry primitive, evasive and ultimately dishonest. Still others have observed that Gray's biography needs 'a fully modern rewriting' – a rewriting which will include a more comprehensive and less prudish discussion of Gray's homoerotic attachments. Gray's conservative biographer R. W. Ketton-Kremer alluded darkly to the unspoken 'secrets of his own nature' which were reawakened by Bonstetten's visit to England in 1771, but failed to pursue the implications of his own intuition with any vigour. He merely noted, for example, that Gray 'knew the existence of temptations which could not for one moment be contemplated by one who had been, all his life long, a strict observer of the laws of God and the laws of men'. Most critics, while acknowledging the 'passionate friendship' which underlies Gray's youthful correspondence with Walpole, as well as the painful attraction obvious in the handful of surviving letters to Bonstetten, stop short of openly discussing Gray as a homosexual writer. Even Roger Lonsdale, one of the best readers Gray has had this century, similarly writes only cryptically of Gray's career as a process to escape 'from a dimly understood sense of a private predicament'. Another critic sympathetic to Gray, Jean Hagstrum, likewise backs off from labelling Gray's (again) 'passionate friendships' with Walpole, West and Bonstetten as homosexual, arguing instead that 'the surviving evidence permits no one to call these and other relationships of Gray overtly homosexual', and moving on (with predictable vagueness) to focus on the 'human intensity' of these friendships.

Such refusal to label Gray's relationships as overtly homosexual is, on one level, justified. I can offer no new evidence of what is euphemistically called 'genital activity' with regard to Gray's personal life which might significantly alter our understanding of Gray the man. Yet I would at the same time suggest that anyone who reads Gray's poetry and correspondence with any degree of sensitivity to its homoerotic subtext *needs* no such evidence. Hagstrum and other critics have argued that we ignore the intensity of Gray's friendships at our critical peril. To ignore the homoeroticism which lies just beneath the surface of Gray's verse is to deny ourselves access to the heart and focus of that emotional intensity, and to deny ourselves access as well to the coherence and consistency of Gray's work. The desire which motivated Gray's homoerotic attachments – his love for Walpole, for West and eventually for Bonstetten – remains the key unspoken signifier beneath all of his poetry. The struggle between the individual sexual will and the forms inhibiting its expression is constantly dramatised in Gray's poetry. The *Elegy* itself acts out the continual activity of reticence and evasion. The poem – with all its babbling, murmuring, lisping, sighing, incoherence, drowsy tinkling, and muted, incomplete acts of communication – privileges obscurity and inarticulation. Indeed, the most striking and memorable articulations of the poem are of those things which are never to be seen – the sensual blush of the desert flower, the gem which remains forever buried in the depths of the ocean. To acknowledge the homoerotic subtext which lurks beneath Gray's poetry is to be able to read *all* of that poetry, for the first time, with real understanding. Such an understanding may enable us to explain why acts of obliquity and reticence remain the focus of the poetry and why parody – with its inherent tactics of indirect allusion and sleight-of-hand mimicry and, more significantly, its method of imitating already-existing structures of self-presentation when no alternative structures exist – remained throughout his entire career such a significant part of Gray's poetic technique.

ROBERT L. MACK

Thomas Gray

Ode on the Spring

Lo! where the rosy-bosom'd Hours,
    Fair Venus' train, appear,
Disclose the long-expecting flowers,
    And wake the purple year!
The Attic warbler pours her throat,
Responsive to the cuckoo's note,
    The untaught harmony of spring:
While, whisp'ring pleasure as they fly,
Cool Zephyrs thro' the clear blue sky
    Their gather'd fragrance fling.   10

Where'er the oak's thick branches stretch
    A broader browner shade,
Where'er the rude and moss-grown beech
    O'er-canopies the glade,
Beside some water's rushy brink
With me the Muse shall sit, and think
    (At ease reclin'd in rustic state)
How vain the ardour of the crowd,
How low, how little are the proud,
    How indigent the great!   20

Still is the toiling hand of Care;
    The panting herds repose:
Yet hark, how thro' the peopled air
    The busy murmur glows!
The insect-youth are on the wing,
Eager to taste the honied spring,
    And float amid the liquid noon:
Some lightly o'er the current skim,
Some show their gayly-gilded trim
    Quick-glancing to the sun.   30

To Contemplation's sober eye
    Such is the race of Man:
And they that creep, and they that fly,

Shall end where they began.
Alike the Busy and the Gay
But flutter thro' life's little day,
    In Fortune's varying colours drest:
Brush'd by the hand of rough Mischance,
Or chill'd by Age, their airy dance
    They leave, in dust to rest.   40

Methinks I hear, in accents low,
    The sportive kind reply:
Poor moralist! and what art thou?
    A solitary fly!
Thy joys no glittering female meets,
No hive hast thou of hoarded sweets,
    No painted plumage to display:
On hasty wings thy youth is flown;
Thy sun is set, thy spring is gone—
    We frolic while 'tis May.   50

Ode on a Distant Prospect of Eton College

Ανθρωπος, ἱκανὴ πρόφαστς εἰς τὸ δυστυχεῖν.

MENANΔEP

Ye distant spires, ye antique towers,
 That crown the wat'ry glade,
Where grateful Science still adores
 Her Henry's holy shade;
And ye, that from the stately brow
Of Windsor's heights th' expanse below
 Of grove, of lawn, of mead survey,
Whose turf, whose shade, whose flowers among
Wanders the hoary Thames along
 His silver-winding way: 10

Ah, happy hills! ah, pleasing shade!
 Ah, fields belov'd in vain!
Where once my careless childhood stray'd,
 A stranger yet to pain!
I feel the gales that from ye blow
A momentary bliss bestow,
 As waving fresh their gladsome wing,
My weary soul they seem to soothe,
And, redolent of joy and youth,
 To breathe a second spring.   20

Say, father Thames, for thou hast seen
 Full many a sprightly race
Disporting on thy margent green,
 The paths of pleasure trace;
Who foremost now delight to cleave,
With pliant arm, thy glassy wave?
 The captive linnet which enthral?
What idle progeny succeed
To chase the rolling circle's speed,
 Or urge the flying ball?   30

While some on earnest business bent
    Their murm'ring labours ply
'Gainst graver hours that bring constraint
    To sweeten liberty:
Some bold adventurers disdain
The limits of their little reign,
    And unknown regions dare descry:
Still as they run they look behind,
They hear a voice in every wind,
    And snatch a fearful joy.   40

Gay hope is theirs by fancy fed,
    Less pleasing when possest;
The tear forgot as soon as shed,
    The sunshine of the breast:
Theirs buxom health, of rosy hue,
Wild wit, invention ever new,
    And lively cheer, of vigour born;
The thoughtless day, the easy night,
The spirits pure, the slumbers light,
    That fly th' approach of morn.   50

Alas! regardless of their doom
    The little victims play;
No sense have they of ills to come,
    Nor care beyond to-day:
Yet see, how all around 'em wait
The ministers of human fate,
    And black Misfortune's baleful train!
Ah, show them where in ambush stand,
To seize their prey, the murth'rous band!
    Ah, tell them, they are men!   60

These shall the fury Passions tear,
    The vultures of the mind,
Disdainful Anger, pallid Fear,
    And Shame that sculks behind;
Or pining Love shall waste their youth,
Or Jealousy, with rankling tooth,
    That inly gnaws the secret heart;

And Envy wan, and faded Care,
Grim-visag'd comfortless Despair,
  And Sorrow's piercing dart.   70

Ambition this shall tempt to rise,
  Then whirl the wretch from high,
To bitter Scorn a sacrifice,
  And grinning Infamy.
The stings of Falsehood those shall try,
And hard Unkindness' alter'd eye,
  That mocks the tear it forc'd to flow;
And keen Remorse with blood defil'd,
And moody Madness laughing wild
  Amid severest woe.   80

Lo! in the vale of years beneath
  A griesly troop are seen,
The painful family of Death,
  More hideous than their queen:
This racks the joints, this fires the veins,
That every labouring sinew strains,
  Those in the deeper vitals rage:
Lo! Poverty, to fill the band,
That numbs the soul with icy hand,
  And slow-consuming Age.   90

To each his suff'rings: all are men,
  Condemn'd alike to groan;
The tender for another's pain,
  Th' unfeeling for his own.
Yet, ah! why should they know their fate,
Since sorrow never comes too late,
  And happiness too swiftly flies?
Thought would destroy their paradise,
No more; – where ignorance is bliss,
  'Tis folly to be wise.   100

Sonnet on the Death of Mr Richard West

In vain to me the smiling mornings shine,
   And redd'ning Phœbus lifts his golden fire:
The birds in vain their amorous descant join;
   Or cheerful fields resume their green attire:
These ears, alas! for other notes repine
   A different object do these eyes require:
My lonely anguish melts no heart but mine;
   And in my breast the imperfect joys expire.
Yet morning smiles the busy race to cheer,
   And new-born pleasure brings to happier men:
The fields to all their wonted tribute bear:
   To warm their little loves the birds complain:
I fruitless mourn to him that cannot hear,
   And weep the more, because I weep in vain.

Ode to Adversity

–Ζῆνα–
. . . .

Τὸν φρονεῖν Βροτὀùς ὁδῷ
σαντα, τῷ πάθει μαθῷν
θέντα κυρίωρ ἔχεὶν. ÆSCH. Agam. ver. 181

Daughter of Jove, relentless power,
  Thou tamer of the human breast,
Whose iron scourge and tort'ring hour
  The bad affright, afflict the best!
  Bound in thy adamantine chain,
  The proud are taught to taste of pain,
  And purple tyrants vainly groan
With pangs unfelt before, unpitied and alone.

When first thy sire to send on earth
  Virtue, his darling child, design'd,   10
To thee he gave the heav'nly birth,
  And bade to form her infant mind.
  Stern rugged nurse! thy rigid lore
  With patience many a year she bore:
  What sorrow was, thou bad'st her know,
And from her own she learn'd to melt at others' woe.

Scar'd at thy frown terrific, fly
  Self-pleasing Folly's idle brood,
Wild Laughter, Noise, and thoughtless Joy,
  And leave us leisure to be good.   20
  Light they disperse, and with them go
  The summer friend, the flattering foe;
  By vain Prosperity receiv'd,
To her they vow their truth, and are again believ'd.

  Wisdom in sable garb array'd,
    Immers'd in rapt'rous thought profound,
  And Melancholy, silent maid,

With leaden eye that loves the ground,
Still on thy solemn steps attend:
Warm Charity, the gen'ral friend,   30
    With Justice, to herself severe,
And Pity, dropping soft the sadly-pleasing tear.

Oh! gently on thy suppliant's head,
    Dread goddess, lay thy chast'ning hand!
Not in thy Gorgon terrors clad,
    Not circled with the vengeful band
(As by the impious thou art seen)
With thund'ring voice, and threat'ning mien,
With screaming Horror's fun'ral cry,
Despair, and fell Disease, and ghastly Poverty: 40

Thy form benign, oh goddess, wear,
    Thy milder influence impart,
Thy philosophic train be there
    To soften, not to wound, my heart.
The gen'rous spark extinct revive
Teach me to love, and to forgive,
Exact my own defects to scan,
What others are to feel, and know myself a Man.   48

Hymn to Ignorance

A Fragment

Hail, horrors, hail! ye ever gloomy bowers,
Ye gothic fanes, and antiquated towers,
Where rushy Camus' slowly-winding flood
Perpetual draws his humid train of mud:
Glad I revisit thy neglected reign,
Oh take me to thy peaceful shade again.
But chiefly thee, whose influence breathed from high,
Augments the native darkness of the sky;
Ah, ignorance! soft salutary power!
Prostrate with filial reverence I adore.   10
Thrice hath Hyperion roll'd his annual race,
Since weeping I forsook thy fond embrace.
Oh say, successful dost thou still oppose
Thy leaden ægis 'gainst our ancient foes?
Still stretch, tenacious of thy right divine,
The massy sceptre o'er thy slumb'ring line?
And dews Lethean through the land dispense
To steep in slumbers each benighted sense?
If any spark of wit's delusive ray
Break out, and flash a momentary day,   20
With damp, cold touch forbid it to aspire,
And huddle up in fogs the dang'rous fire.
     Oh say – she hears me not, but, careless grown,
Lethargic nods upon her ebon throne.
Goddess! awake, arise! alas, my fears!
Can powers immortal feel the force of years?
Not thus of old, with ensigns wide unfurl'd,
She rode triumphant o'er the vanquish'd world;
Fierce Nations own'd her unresisted might,
And all was ignorance, and all was night.   30
     Oh! sacred age! Oh! times for ever lost!
(The schoolman's glory, and the churchman's boast.)
For ever gone – yet still to fancy new,
Her rapid wings the transient scene pursue,
And bring the buried ages back to view.

High on her car, behold the grandam ride
Like old Sesostris with barbaric pride;
. . . a team of harness'd monarchs bend

Ode on the Death of a Favourite Cat, Drowned in a Tub of Gold Fishes

'Twas on a lofty vase's side,
Where China's gayest art had dy'd
   The azure flowers, that blow;
Demurest of the tabby kind,
The pensive Selima, reclin'd,
   Gaz'd on the lake below.

Her conscious tail her joy declar'd;
The fair round face, the snowy beard,
   The velvet of her paws,
Her coat, that with the tortoise vies,   10
Her ears of jet, and emerald eyes,
   She saw; and purr'd applause,

Still had she gaz'd; but 'midst the tide
Two angel forms were seen to glide,
   The Genii of the stream:
Their scaly armour's Tyrian hue
Through richest purple to the view
   Betray'd a golden gleam.

The hapless nymph with wonder saw:
A whisker first, and then a claw,   20
   With many an ardent wish,
She stretch'd, in vain, to reach the prize,
What female heart can gold despise?
   What Cat's averse to fish?

Presumptuous maid! with looks intent
Again she stretch'd, again she bent,
   Nor knew the gulf between.
(Malignant Fate sat by, and smil'd)
The slipp'ry verge her feet beguil'd,
   She tumbled headlong in.   30

Eight times emerging from the flood
She mew'd to ev'ry wat'ry God,
   Some speedy aid to send.
No Dolphin came, no Nereid stirr'd:
Nor cruel Tom, nor Susan heard.
   A fav'rite has no friend!

From hence, ye beauties, undeceiv'd,
Know, one false step is ne'er retriev'd,
   And be with caution bold.
Not all that tempts your wand'ring eyes   40
And heedless hearts is lawful prize,
   Nor all that glisters, gold.

Elegy Written in a Country Churchyard

The curfew tolls the knell of parting day,
  The lowing herd winds slowly o'er the lea,
The ploughman homeward plods his weary way,
  And leaves the world to darkness and to me.

Now fades the glimmering landscape on the sight,
  And all the air a solemn stillness holds,
Save where the beetle wheels his droning flight,
  And drowsy tinklings lull the distant folds:

Save that from yonder ivy-mantled tow'r,
  The moping owl does to the moon complain   10
Of such as, wand'ring near her secret bow'r,
  Molest her ancient solitary reign.

Beneath those rugged elms, that yew-tree's shade,
  Where heaves the turf in many a mould'ring heap,
Each in his narrow cell for ever laid,
  The rude forefathers of the hamlet sleep.

The breezy call of incense-breathing morn,
  The swallow twitt'ring from the straw-built shed,
The cock's shrill clarion, or the echoing horn,
  No more shall rouse them from their lowly bed.   20

For them no more the blazing hearth shall burn,
  Or busy housewife ply her evening care;
No children run to lisp their sire's return,
  Or climb his knees the envied kiss to share.

Oft did the harvest to their sickle yield,
  Their furrow oft the stubborn glebe has broke:
How jocund did they drive their team afield!
  How bow'd the woods beneath their sturdy stroke!

Let not ambition mock their useful toil,
  Their homely joys, and destiny obscure;   30

Nor grandeur hear with a disdainful smile
　　The short and simple annals of the poor.

The boast of heraldry, the pomp of pow'r,
　　And all that beauty, all that wealth e'er gave,
Awaits alike th' inevitable hour.
　　The paths of glory lead but to the grave.

Nor you, ye proud, impute to these the fault,
　　If memory o'er their tomb no trophies raise,
Where through the long-drawn aisle and fretted vault
　　The pealing anthem swells the note of praise.   40

Can storied urn, or animated bust,
　　Back to its mansion call the fleeting breath?
Can honour's voice provoke the silent dust,
　　Or flatt'ry soothe the dull cold ear of death?

Perhaps in this neglected spot is laid
　　Some heart once pregnant with celestial fire;
Hands, that the rod of empire might have sway'd,
　　Or wak'd to extasy the living lyre.

But knowledge to their eyes her ample page
　　Rich with the spoils of time did ne'er unroll;   50
'Chill penury repress'd their noble rage,'
　　And froze the genial current of the soul.

Full many a gem of purest ray serene
　　The dark unfathom'd caves of ocean bear:
Full many a flower is born to blush unseen,
　　And waste its sweetness on the desert air.

Some village Hampden, that, with dauntless breast,
　　The little tyrant of his fields withstood,
Some mute inglorious Milton here may rest,
　　Some Cromwell guiltless of his country's blood.   60

Th' applause of list'ning senates to command,
　　The threats of pain and ruin to despise,

To scatter plenty o'er a smiling land,
   And read their history in a nation's eyes,

Their lot forbad: nor circumscrib'd alone
   Their growing virtues, but their crimes confined
Forbad to wade thro' slaughter to a throne,
   And shut the gates of mercy on mankind,

The struggling pangs of conscious truth to hide,
   To quench the blushes of ingenuous shame,   70
Or heap the shrine of luxury and pride
   With incense kindled at the Muse's flame.

Far from the madding crowd's ignoble strife,
   Their sober wishes never learn'd to stray;
Along the cool sequester'd vale of life
   They kept the noiseless tenour of their way.

Yet ev'n these bones from insult to protect
   Some frail memorial still erected nigh,
With uncouth rhymes and shapeless sculpture deck'd,
   Implores the passing tribute of a sigh.   80

Their name, their years, spelt by th' unletter'd Muse,
   The place of fame and elegy supply:
And many a holy text around she strews,
   That teach the rustic moralist to die.

For who, to dumb forgetfulness a prey,
   This pleasing anxious being e'er resign'd,
Left the warm precincts of the cheerful day,
   Nor cast one longing ling'ring look behind?

On some fond breast the parting soul relies,
   Some pious drops the closing eye requires;   90
E'en from the tomb the voice of nature cries,
   E'en in our ashes live their wonted fires.

For thee, who, mindful of th' unhonour'd dead,
   Dost in these lines their artless tale relate;

If chance, by lonely contemplation led,
    Some kindred spirit shall enquire thy fate,—

Haply some hoary-headed swain may say,
    'Oft have we seen him at the peep of dawn
Brushing with hasty steps the dews away,
    To meet the sun upon the upland lawn.   100

'There at the foot of yonder nodding beech,
    That wreathes its old fantastic roots so high,
His listless length at noontide would he stretch,
    And pore upon the brook that babbles by.

'Hard by yon wood, now smiling as in scorn,
    Mutt'ring his wayward fancies he would rove;
Now drooping, woful-wan, like one forlorn,
    Or craz'd with care, or cross'd in hopeless love.

'One morn I miss'd him on the custom'd hill,
    Along the heath, and near his fav'rite tree;   110
Another came; nor yet beside the rill,
    Nor up the lawn, nor at the wood was he:

'The next, with dirges due in sad array
    Slow through the church-way path we saw him borne:—
Approach and read (for thou can'st read) the lay
    Grav'd on the stone beneath yon aged thorn.'

THE EPITAPH

Here rests his head upon the lap of earth
    A youth, to fortune and to fame unknown;
Fair science frown'd not on his humble birth,
    And melancholy mark'd him for her own.   120

Large was his bounty, and his soul sincere,
    Heaven did a recompense as largely send:
He gave to mis'ry (all he had) a tear,
    He gain'd from heav'n ('twas all he wish'd) a friend.

No farther seek his merits to disclose,
    Or draw his frailties from their dread abode
(There they alike in trembling hope repose),
    The bosom of his Father and his God.

A Long Story

In Britain's isle, no matter where,
    An ancient pile of building stands:
The Huntingdons and Hattons there
    Employ'd the pow'r of fairy hands

To raise the ceiling's fretted height,
    Each pannel in achievements clothing,
Rich windows that exclude the light,
    And passages, that lead to nothing.

Full oft within the spacious walls,
    When he had fifty winters o'er him,   10
My grave Lord-Keeper led the brawls;
    The seals and maces danc'd before him.

His bushy beard, and shoe-strings green,
    His high-crown'd hat, and satin doublet,
Mov'd the stout heart of England's queen,
    Though Pope and Spaniard could not trouble it.

What, in the very first beginning!
    Shame of the versifying tribe!
Your hist'ry whither are you spinning!
    Can you do nothing but describe?   20

A house there is (and that's enough)
    From whence one fatal morning issues
A brace of warriors, not in buff,
    But rustling in their silks and tissues.

The first came cap-a-pee from France,
    Her conqu'ring destiny fulfilling,
Whom meaner beauties eye askance,
    And vainly ape her art of killing.

The other amazon kind heav'n
    Had arm'd with spirit, wit, and satire;   30

But Cobham had the polish giv'n,
    And tipp'd her arrows with good-nature.

To celebrate her eyes, her air—
    Coarse panegyrics would but tease her;
Melissa is her 'nom de guerre.'
    Alas, who would not wish to please her!

With bonnet blue and capuchine,
    And aprons long, they hid their armour;
And veil'd their weapons, bright and keen,
    In pity to the country farmer.   40

Fame, in the shape of Mr P—t
    (By this time all the parish know it),
Had told that thereabouts there lurk'd
    A wicked imp they call a poet:

Who prowl'd the country far and near,
    Bewitch'd the children of the peasants,
Dried up the cows, and lam'd the deer,
    And suck'd the eggs, and kill'd the pheasants.

My lady heard their joint petition,
    Swore by her coronet and ermine,   50
She'd issue out her high commission
    To rid the manor of such vermin.

The heroines undertook the task,
    Thro' lanes unknown, o'er stiles they ventur'd,
Rapp'd at the door, nor stay'd to ask,
    But bounce into the parlour enter'd.

The trembling family they daunt,
    They flirt, they sing, they laugh, they tattle,
Rummage his mother, pinch his aunt,
    And upstairs in a whirlwind rattle: 60

Each hole and cupboard they explore,
    Each creek and cranny of his chamber,

Run hurry-scurry round the floor,
　　And o'er the bed and tester clamber;

Into the drawers and china pry,
　　Papers and books, a huge imbroglio!
Under a tea-cup he might lie,
　　Or creased, like dog-ears, in a folio.

On the first marching of the troops,
　　The Muses, hopeless of his pardon,   70
Convey'd him underneath their hoops
　　To a small closet in the garden.

So rumour says (who will, believe);
　　But that they left the door ajar,
Where, safe and laughing in his sleeve,
　　He heard the distant din of war.

Short was his joy. He little knew
　　The pow'r of magic was no fable;
Out of the window, wisk, they flew,
　　But left a spell upon the table.   80

The words too eager to unriddle,
　　The poet felt a strange disorder;
Transparent bird-lime form'd the middle,
　　And chains invisible the border.

So cunning was the apparatus,
　　The powerful pot-hooks did so move him,
That, will he, nill he, to the great house
　　He went, as if the devil drove him.

Yet on his way (no sign of grace,
　　For folks in fear are apt to pray)   90
To Phœbus he preferr'd his case,
　　And begg'd his aid that dreadful day.

The godhead would have back'd his quarrel;
　　But with a blush, on recollection,

Own'd that his quiver and his laurel
   'Gainst four such eyes were no protection.

The court was sate, the culprit there,
   Forth from their gloomy mansions creeping
The lady Janes and Joans repair,
   And from the gallery stand peeping: 100

Such as in silence of the night
   Come (sweep) along some winding entry
(Styack has often seen the sight),
   Or at the chapel-door stand sentry:

In peaked hoods and mantles tarnish'd,
   Sour visages, enough to scare ye,
High dames of honour once, that garnish'd
   The drawing-room of fierce Queen Mary.

The peeress comes. The audience stare,
   And doff their hats with due submission: 110
She curtsies, as she takes her chair,
   To all the people of condition.

The bard, with many an artful fib,
   Had in imagination fenc'd him,
Disprov'd the arguments of Squib,
   And all that Groom could urge against him.

But soon his rhetoric forsook him,
   When he the solemn hall had seen;
A sudden fit of ague shook him,
   He stood as mute as poor Macleane.   120

Yet something he was heard to mutter,
   'How in the park beneath an old tree,
(Without design to hurt the butter
   Or any malice to the poultry),

'He once or twice had penn'd a sonnet;
   Yet hop'd, that he might save his bacon:

Numbers would give their oaths upon it,
   He ne'er was for a conj'rer taken.'

The ghostly prudes with hagged face
   Already had condemn'd the sinner.   130
My lady rose, and with a grace—
   She smil'd, and bid him come to dinner.

'Jesu-Maria! Madam Bridget,
   Why, what can the Viscountess mean?'
(Cried the square-hoods in woful fidget)
   'The times are alter'd quite and clean!

'Decorum's turn'd to mere civility;
   Her air and all her manners show it.
Commend me to her affability!
   Speak to a commoner and poet!'   140

          [Here five hundred stanzas are lost.]

And so God save our noble king,
   And guard us from long-winded lubbers,
That to eternity would sing,
   And keep my lady from her rubbers.

The Progress of Poesy

A Pindaric Ode

Φωνᾶντα συνετοῖσιν. ἐς
Δὲ τὸ πᾶν ἑρμηνέων
Χατίζει. – PINDAR, Ol. ii. v. 152.

I. 1

Awake, Æolian lyre, awake,
And give to rapture all thy trembling strings.
From Helicon's harmonious springs
   A thousand rills their mazy progress take:
The laughing flowers that round them blow,
Drink life and fragrance as they flow.
Now the rich stream of music winds along,
Deep, majestic, smooth, and strong,
Thro' verdant vales, and Ceres' golden reign:
Now rolling down the steep amain,   10
Headlong, impetuous, see it pour;
The rocks and nodding groves rebellow to the roar.

I. 2

   Oh! Sov'reign of the willing soul,
Parent of sweet and solemn-breathing airs,
Enchanting shell! the sullen Cares
   And frantic Passions hear thy soft controul,
On Thracia's hills the Lord of War
Has curb'd the fury of his car,
And dropt his thirsty lance at thy command.
Perching on the scept'red hand   20
Of Jove, thy magic lulls the feather'd king
With ruffled plumes and flagging wing:
Quench'd in dark clouds of slumber lie
The terror of his beak, and lightnings of his eye.

I. 3

Thee the voice, the dance, obey,
Temper'd to thy warbled lay.

O'er Idalia's velvet-green
The rosy-crowned Loves are seen
On Cytherea's day;
With antic Sport, and blue-eyed Pleasures,   30
Frisking light in frolic measures;
Now pursuing, now retreating,
    Now in circling troops they meet:
To brisk notes in cadence beating,
    Glance their many-twinkling feet.
Slow melting strains their Queen's approach declare:
    Where'er she turns, the Graces homage pay.
With arm sublime, that float upon the air,
    In gliding state she wins her easy way:
O'er her warm cheek, and rising bosom, move   40
The bloom of young Desire and purple light of Love.

II. 1

    Man's feeble race what ills await!
Labour, and Penury, the racks of Pain,
Disease, and Sorrow's weeping train,
    And Death, sad refuge from the storms of fate!
The fond complaint, my song, disprove,
And justify the laws of Jove.
Say, has he giv'n in vain the heav'nly Muse?
Night and all her sickly dews,
Her spectres wan, and birds of boding cry,   50
He gives to range the dreary sky;
Till down the eastern cliffs afar
Hyperion's march they spy, and glitt'ring shafts of war.

II. 2

    In climes beyond the solar road,
Where shaggy forms o'er ice-built mountains roam,
The Muse has broke the twilight gloom
    To cheer the shivering native's dull abode.
And oft, beneath the od'rous shade
Of Chili's boundless forests laid,
She deigns to hear the savage youth repeat,   60
In loose numbers wildly sweet,
Their feather-cinctur'd chiefs, and dusky loves.

Her track, where'er the goddess roves,
Glory pursue, and gen'rous Shame,
Th' unconquerable Mind, and freedom's holy flame.

II. 3

Woods, that wave o'er Delphi's steep,
Isles, that crown th' Ægean deep,
　Fields, that cool Ilissus laves,
　Or where Mæander's amber waves
In lingering lab'rinths creep,   70
　How do your tuneful echoes languish,
　Mute, but to the voice of anguish!
Where each old poetic mountain
　Inspiration breath'd around;
Ev'ry shade and hallow'd fountain
　Murmur'd deep a solemn sound:
Till the sad Nine, in Greece's evil hour,
　Left their Parnassus for the Latian plains.
Alike they scorn the pomp of tyrant Power,
　And coward Vice, that revels in her chains.   80
When Latium had her lofty spirit lost,
They sought, oh Albion! next thy sea-encircled coast.

III. 1

Far from the sun and summer-gale,
In thy green lap was Nature's Darling laid,
What time, where lucid Avon stray'd,
　To him the mighty mother did unveil
Her awful face: the dauntless child
Stretch'd forth his little arms and smil'd,
'This pencil take (she said), whose colours clear
Richly paint the vernal year: 90
Thine too these golden keys, immortal Boy!
This can unlock the gates of joy;
Of horror that, and thrilling fears,
Or ope the sacred source of sympathetic tears.'

III. 2

Nor second He, that rode sublime
Upon the seraph-wings of Extasy,

The secrets of th' abyss to spy.
    He pass'd the flaming bounds of place and time:
The living throne, the sapphire blaze,
Where angels tremble while they gaze,   100
He saw; but, blasted with excess of light,
Clos'd his eyes in endless night.
Behold, where Dryden's less presumptuous car,
Wide o'er the fields of glory bear
Two coursers of ethereal race,
With necks in thunder cloth'd, and long-resounding pace,

3. 3

    Hark, his hands the lyre explore!
Bright-eyed Fancy, hov'ring o'er,
Scatters from her pictur'd urn
Thoughts that breathe, and words that burn.   110
But ah! 'tis heard no more—
    Oh! lyre divine, what daring spirit
    Wakes thee now? Tho' he inherit
Nor the pride, nor ample pinion,
    That the Theban eagle bear,
Sailing with supreme dominion
    Thro' the azure deep of air:
Yet oft before his infant eyes would run
    Such forms as glitter in the Muse's ray,
With orient hues, unborrow'd of the sun: 120
    Yet shall he mount, and keep his distant way
Beyond the limits of a vulgar fate,
Beneath the Good how far – but far above the Great.

The Bard

A Pindaric Ode

I. 1

'Ruin seize thee, ruthless King!
   Confusion on thy banners wait;
Tho' fann'd by Conquest's crimson wing,
   They mock the air with idle state.
Helm, nor hauberk's twisted mail,
Nor e'en thy virtues, Tyrant, shall avail
   To save thy secret soul from nightly fears,
   From Cambria's curse, from Cambria's tears!'
Such were the sounds that o'er the crested pride
   Of the first Edward scatter'd wild dismay,   10
As down the steep of Snowdon's shaggy side
   He wound with toilsome march his long array.
Stout Glo'ster stood aghast in speechless trance:
'To arms!' cried Mortimer, and couch'd his quiv'ring lance,

I. 2

On a rock, whose haughty brow
Frowns o'er cold Conway's foaming flood,
   Robed in the sable garb of woe,
With haggard eyes the poet stood;
(Loose his beard, and hoary hair
Stream'd, like a meteor, to the troubled air)   20
And with a master's hand, and prophet's fire,
Struck the deep sorrows of his lyre.
   'Hark, how each giant-oak, and desert cave,
Sighs to the torrent's awful voice beneath!
O'er thee, oh King! their hundred arms they wave,
   Revenge on thee in hoarser murmurs breathe;
Vocal no more, since Cambria's fatal day,
To high-born Hoel's harp, or soft Llewellyn's lay.

I. 3

   'Cold is Cadwallo's tongue,
That hush'd the story main: 30

Brave Urien sleeps upon his craggy bed:
   Mountains, ye mourn in vain
   Modred, whose magic song
Made huge Plinlimmon bow his cloud-topt head.
   On dreary Arvon's shore they lie,
Smear'd with gore, and ghastly pale:
Far, far aloof th' affrighted ravens sail;
   The famish'd eagle screams, and passes by.
Dear lost companions of my tuneful art,
   Dear as the light that visits these sad eyes,   40
Dear as the ruddy drops that warm my heart,
   Ye died amidst your dying country's cries—
No more I weep. They do not sleep.
   On yonder cliffs, a griesly band,
I see them sit, they linger yet,
   Avengers of their native land:
With me in dreadful harmony they join,
And weave with bloody hands the tissue of thy line.

II. 1

   'Weave the warp, and weave the woof,
The winding-sheet of Edward's race.   50
   Give ample room, and verge enough
The characters of hell to trace.
Mark the year, and mark the night,
When Severn shall re-echo with affright
The shrieks of death, thro' Berkley's roof that ring,
Shrieks of an agonising king!
   She-wolf of France, with unrelenting fangs,
That tear'st the bowels of thy mangled mate,
   From thee be born, who o'er thy country hangs
The scourge of heav'n. What terrors round him wait!   60
Amazement in his van, with flight combin'd,
And sorrow's faded form, and solitude behind.

II. 2

   'Mighty victor, mighty lord!
Low on his funeral couch he lies!
   No pitying heart, no eye, afford

A tear to grace his obsequies.
    Is the sable warrior fled?
Thy son is gone. He rests among the dead.
The swarm, that in thy noontide beam were born?
Gone to salute the rising morn.   70
Fair laughs the morn, and soft the zephyr blows,
    While proudly riding o'er the azure realm
In gallant trim the gilded vessel goes;
    Youth on the prow, and Pleasure at the helm;
Regardless of the sweeping whirlwind's sway,
That, hush'd in grim repose, expects his ev'ning prey.

II. 3
    'Fill high the sparkling bowl,
The rich repast prepare,
    Reft of a crown, he yet may share the feast:
Close by the regal chair   80
    Fell Thirst and Famine scowl
    A baleful smile upon their baffled guest.
Heard ye the din of battle bray,
    Lance to lance, and horse to horse?
    Long years of havock urge their destined course,
And thro' the kindred squadrons mow their way.
    Ye towers of Julius, London's lasting shame,
With many a foul and midnight murder fed,
    Revere his consort's faith, his father's fame,
And spare the meek usurper's holy head.   90
Above, below, the rose of snow,
    Twin'd with her blushing foe, we spread:
The bristled boar in infant-gore
    Wallows beneath the thorny shade.
Now, brothers, bending o'er the accursed loom,
Stamp we our vengeance deep, and ratify his doom.

III. 1
    'Edward, lo! to sudden fate
(Weave we the woof. The thread is spun.)
    Half of thy heart we consecrate.
(The web is wove. The work is done.)   100
Stay, oh stay! nor thus forlorn

Leave me unbless'd, unpitied, here to mourn:
In yon bright track, that fires the western skies,
They melt, they vanish from my eyes.
But oh! what solemn scenes on Snowdon's height
   Descending slow their glittering skirts unroll?
Visions of glory, spare my aching sight!
   Ye unborn ages, crowd not on my soul!
No more our long-lost Arthur we bewail.
All hail, ye genuine kings, Britannia's issue, hail!   120

III. 2

'Girt with many a baron bold
Sublime their starry fronts they rear;
   And gorgeous dames, and statesmen old
In bearded majesty, appear.
In the midst a form divine!
Her eye proclaims her of the Briton-line;
Her lion-port, her awe-commanding face,
Attemper'd sweet to virgin-grace.
What strings symphonious tremble in the air,
   What strains of vocal transport round her play.   130
Hear from the grave, great Taliessin, hear;
   They breathe a soul to animate thy clay.
Bright Rapture calls, and soaring as she sings,
Waves in the eye of heav'n her many-colour'd wings.

III. 3

'The verse adorn again
   Fierce war, and faithful love,
And truth severe, by fairy fiction drest.
   In buskin'd measures move
Pale grief, and pleasing pain,
With horror, tyrant of the throbbing breast.   140
   A voice, as of the cherub-choir,
Gales from blooming Eden bear;
And distant warblings lessen on my ear,
   That lost in long futurity expire.
Fond impious man, think'st thou yon sanguine cloud,
   Rais'd by thy breath, has quench'd the orb of day?
To-morrow he repairs the golden flood,

And warms the nations with redoubled ray.
Enough for me; with joy I see
  The diff'rent doom our fates assign.   150
Be thine despair, and scept'red care,
  To triumph, and to die, are mine.'
He spoke, and headlong from the mountain's height
Deep in the roaring tide he plunged to endless night.

Ode on the Pleasure Arising From Vicissitude

Now the golden morn aloft
   Waves her dew-bespangled wing.
With vermeil cheek and whisper soft
   She wooes the tardy spring:
Till April starts, and calls around
The sleeping fragrance from the ground;
And lightly o'er the living scene
Scatters his freshest, tenderest green.

New-born flocks, in rustic dance,
   Frisking ply their feeble feet;   10
Forgetful of their wintry trance
   The birds his presence greet:
But chief, the sky-lark warbles high
His trembling thrilling extasy;
And, lessening from the dazzled sight,
Melts into air and liquid light.

Rise, my soul! on wings of fire,
   Rise the rapt'rous choir among;
Hark! 'tis nature strikes the lyre,
   And leads the gen'ral song: 20
.   .   .   .
Yesterday the sullen year
   Saw the snowy whirlwind fly;
Mute was the music of the air,
   The herd stood drooping by:
Their raptures now that wildly flow,
No yesterday nor morrow know;
'Tis man alone that joy descries
With forward, and reverted eyes.

Smiles on past misfortune's brow
   Soft reflection's hand can trace;   30

And o'er the cheek of sorrow throw
   A melancholy grace;
While hope prolongs our happier hour,
Or deepest shades, that dimly lower
And blacken round our weary way,
Gilds with a gleam of distant day.

Still, where rosy pleasure leads,
   See a kindred grief pursue;
Behind the steps that misery treads,
   Approaching comfort view: 40
The hues of bliss more brightly glow,
Chastis'd by sabler tints of woe;
And blended form, with artful strife,
The strength and harmony of life.

See the wretch, that long has tost
   On the thorny bed of pain,
At length repair his vigour lost,
   And breathe and walk again:
The meanest floweret of the vale,
The simplest note that swells the gale,   50
The common sun, the air, the skies,
To him are opening paradise.

Humble quiet builds her cell,
   Near the source whence pleasure flows;
She eyes the clear crystalline well,
   And tastes it as it goes.

Epitaph on Mrs Clerke

Lo! where this silent marble weeps,
A friend, a wife, a mother sleeps:
A heart, within whose sacred cell
The peaceful virtues lov'd to dwell.
Affection warm, and faith sincere,
And soft humanity were there.
In agony, in death resign'd,
She felt the wound she left behind,
Her infant image here below,
Sits smiling on a father's woe:
Whom what awaits, while yet he strays
Along the lonely vale of days?
A pang, to secret sorrow dear;
A sigh; an unavailing tear;
Till time shall every grief remove,
With life, with memory, and with love.

Epitaph On A Child

Here, free'd from pain, secure from misery, lies
A Child the Darling of his Parent's eyes:
A gentler Lamb ne'er sported on the plain,
A fairer Flower will never bloom again!
Few were the days allotted to his breath;
Here let him sleep in peace his night of death.

The Fatal Sisters

An Ode. From the Norse Tongue

PREFACE

In the eleventh century Sigurd, Earl of the Orkney Islands, went with a fleet of ships and a considerable body of troops into Ireland, to the assistance of Sictryg with the silken beard, who was then making war on his father-in-law Brian, King of Dublin: the Earl and all his forces were cut to pieces, and Sictryg was in danger of a total defeat; but the enemy had a greater loss by the death of Brian, their King, who fell in the action. On Christmas-day (the day of the battle), a native of Caithness in Scotland saw at a distance a number of persons on horseback riding full speed towards a hill, and seeming to enter into it. Curiosity led him to follow them, till looking through an opening in the rocks he saw twelve gigantic figures resembling women: they were all employed about a loom; and as they wove, they sung the following dreadful song; which when they had finished, they tore the web into twelve pieces, and (each taking her portion) galloped six to the north and as many to the south.

> Now the storm begins to lower
>   (Haste, the loom of hell prepare),
> Iron sleet of arrowy shower
>   Hurtles in the darken'd air.
>
> Glitt'ring lances are the loom,
>   Where the dusky warp we strain,
> Weaving many a soldier's doom,
>   Orkney's woe, and Randver's bane.
>
> See the griesly texture grow!
>   ('Tis of human entrails made)
> And the weights, that play below,
>   Each a gasping warrior's head.
>
> Shafts for shuttles, dipt in gore,
>   Shoot the trembling cords along.

10

Sword, that once a monarch bore,
    Keep the tissue close and strong.

Mista, black terrific maid,
    Sangrida, and Hilda, see,
Join the wayward work to aid:
    'Tis the woof of victory.   20

Ere the ruddy sun be set,
    Pikes must shiver, javelins sing,
Blade with clattering buckler meet,
    Hauberk crash, and helmet ring.

(Weave the crimson web of war)
    Let us go, and let us fly,
Where our friends the conflict share,
    Where they triumph, where they die.

As the paths of fate we tread,
    Wading through th' ensanguin'd field,   30
Gondula, and Geira, spread
    O'er the youthful king your shield.

We the reins to slaughter give,
    Ours to kill, and ours to spare:
Spite of danger he shall live.
    (Weave the crimson web of war.)

They, whom once the desert-beach
    Pent within its bleak domain,
Soon their ample sway shall stretch
    O'er the plenty of the plain.   40

Low the dauntless earl is laid,
    Gor'd with many a gaping wound:
Fate demands a nobler head;
    Soon a king shall bite the ground.

Long his loss shall Eirin weep,
    Ne'er again his likeness see;

Long her strains in sorrow steep:
   Strains of immortality!

Horror covers all the heath,
   Clouds of carnage blot the sun,   50
Sisters, weave the web of death;
   Sisters, cease; the work is done.

Hail the task, and hail the hands!
   Songs of joy and triumph sing!
Joy to the victorious bands;
   Triumph to the younger king.

Mortal, thou that hear'st the tale,
   Learn the tenour of our song.
Scotland, thro' each winding vale
   Far and wide the notes prolong.   60

Sisters, hence with spurs of speed:
   Each her thundering faulchion wield;
Each bestride her sable steed.
   Hurry, hurry to the field!

The Descent of Odin

An Ode. From the Norse Tongue

Uprose the king of men with speed,
And saddled straight his coal-black steed;
Down the yawning steep he rode,
That leads to Hela's drear abode.
Him the dog of darkness spied;
His shaggy throat he open'd wide
(While from his jaws, with carnage fill'd,
Foam and human gore distill'd):
Hoarse he bays with hideous din,
Eyes that glow, and fangs that grin;   10
And long pursues with fruitless yell,
The father of the powerful spell.
Onward still his way he takes
(The groaning earth beneath him shakes),
Till full before his fearless eyes
The portals nine of hell arise.

Right against the eastern gate,
By the moss-grown pile he sate;
Where long of yore to sleep was laid
The dust of the prophetic maid.   20
Facing to the northern clime,
Thrice he trac'd the Runic rhyme;
Thrice pronounc'd, in accents dread,
The thrilling verse that wakes the dead:
Till from out the hollow ground
Slowly breath'd a sullen sound.

PROPHETESS
What call unknown, what charms presume
To break the quiet of the tomb?
Who thus afflicts my troubled sprite,

And drags me from the realms of night?   30
Long on these mould'ring bones have beat
The winter's snow, the summer's heat,
The drenching dews, and driving rain!
Let me, let me sleep again.
Who is he, with voice unblest,
That calls me from the bed of rest?

ODIN
A traveller, to thee unknown,
Is he that calls, a warrior's son.
Thou the deeds of light shalt know;
Tell me what is done below,   40
For whom yon glitt'ring board is spread,
Dress'd for whom yon golden bed?

PROPHETESS
Mantling in the goblet see
The pure bev'rage of the bee:
O'er it hangs the shield of gold;
'Tis the drink of Balder bold:
Balder's head to death is giv'n.
Pain can reach the sons of heav'n!
Unwilling I my lips unclose:
Leave me, leave me to repose.   50

ODIN
Once again my call obey,
Prophetess, arise, and say,
What dangers Odin's child await,
Who the author of his fate?

PROPHETESS
In Hoder's hand the hero's doom;
His brother sends him to the tomb.
Now my weary lips I close:
Leave me, leave me to repose.

ODIN
Prophetess, my spell obey,
Once again arise, and say,   60

Who th' avenger of his guilt,
By whom shall Hoder's blood be spilt?

PROPHETESS
In the caverns of the west,
By Odin's fierce embrace comprest,
A wond'rous boy shall Rinda bear,
Who ne'er shall comb his raven-hair,
Nor wash his visage in the stream,
Nor see the sun's departing beam,
Till he on Hoder's corse shall smile
Flaming on the fun'ral pile.   70
Now my weary lips I close:
Leave me, leave me to repose.

ODIN
Yet a while my call obey;
Prophetess, awake, and say,
What virgins these, in speechless woe,
That bend to earth their solemn brow,
That their flaxen tresses fear,
And snowy veils that float in air?
Tell me whence their sorrows rose:
Then I leave thee to repose.   80

PROPHETESS
Ha! no traveller art thou,
King of men, I know thee now;
Mightiest of a mighty line—

ODIN
No boding maid of skill divine
Art thou, nor prophetess of good;
But mother of the giant brood!

PROPHETESS
Hie thee hence, and boast at home,
That never shall enquirer come
To break my iron-sleep again;
Till Lok has burst his tenfold chain;   90

Never, till substantial night
Has reassum'd her ancient right;
Till wrapt in flames, in ruin hurl'd,
Sinks the fabric of the world.

The Triumphs of Owen

A Fragment. From the Welsh

Owen's praise demands my song,
Owen swift, and Owen strong;
Fairest flower of Roderic's stem,
Gwyneth's shield, and Britain's gem.
He nor heaps his brooded stores,
Nor on all profusely pours;
Lord of every regal art,
Liberal hand, and open heart.
Big with hosts of mighty name,
Squadrons three against him came;   10
This the force of Eirin hiding,
Side by side as proudly riding,
On her shadow long and gay
Lochlin plows the wat'ry way;
There the Norman sails afar
Catch the winds and join the war:
Black and huge along they sweep,
Burthens of the angry deep.

    Dauntless on his native sands
The dragon-son of Mona stands;   20
In glitt'ring arms and glory drest,
High he rears his ruby crest.
There the thund'ring strokes begin,
There the press, and there the din;
Talymalfra's rocky shore
Echoing to the battle's roar.
Check'd by the torrent-tide of blood,
Backward Meinai rolls his flood;
While, heap'd his master's feet around,
Prostrate warriors gnaw the ground.   30
Where his glowing eye-balls turn,
Thousand banners round him burn:
Where he points his purple spear,

Hasty, hasty rout is there,
Marking with indignant eye
Fear to stop, and shame to fly.
There confusion, terror's child,
Conflict fierce, and ruin wild,
Agony, that pants for breath,
Despair and honourable death.   40

Sketch of his Own Character

Too poor for a bribe, and too proud to importune;
He had not the method of making a fortune:
Could love, and could hate, so was thought somewhat odd;
No very great wit, he believed in a God:
A post or a pension he did not desire,
But left church and state to Charles Townshend and Squire.

Song I

(''Midst beauty and pleasure's
gay triumphs, to languish')

'Midst beauty and pleasure's gay triumphs, to languish
And droop without knowing the source of my anguish;
To start from short slumbers and look for the morning—
Yet close my dull eyes when I see it returning;

Sighs sudden and frequent, looks ever dejected,
Sounds that steal from my tongue, by no meaning connected!
Ah say, fellow-swains, how these symptoms befell me?
They smile, but reply not. Sure Delia will tell me!

Song II

('Thyris, when we parted, swore')

Thyrsis, when we parted, swore
   Ere the spring he would return—
Ah! what means yon violet flower!
   And the bud that decks the thorn!
'Twas the lark that upward sprung!
'Twas the nightingale that sung!

Idle notes! untimely green!
   Why this unavailing haste?
Western gales and skies serene
   Speak not always winter past.
Cease, my doubts, my fears to move,
   Spare the honour of my love.

The Candidate

or, The Cambridge Courtship

When sly Jenny Twitcher had smugg'd up his face,
With a lick of court white-wash, and pious grimace,
A wooing he went, where three sisters of old
In harmless society guttle and scold.
    'Lord! sister,' says Physic to Law, 'I declare
Such a sheep-biting look, such a pick-pocket air!
Not I for the Indies: – You know I'm no prude,—
But his nose is a shame, – and his eyes are so lewd!
Then he shambles and straddles so oddly – I fear—
No – at our time of life 'twould be silly, my dear.'   10
    'I don't know,' says Law, 'but methinks for his look,
'Tis just like the picture in Rochester's book;
Then his character, Phyzzy – his morals – his life –
When she died, I can't tell, but he once had a wife.
They say he's no Christian, loves drinking and w——g,
And all the town rings of his swearing and roaring!
His lying and filching, and Newgate-bird tricks;—
Not I – for a coronet, chariot and six.'
    Divinity heard, between waking and dozing,
Her sisters denying, and Jemmy proposing: 20
From table she rose, and with bumper in hand,
She strok'd up her belly, and strok'd down her band—
'What a pother is here about wenching and roaring!
Why, David lov'd catches, and Solomon w——g:
Did not Israel filch from th' Egyptians of old
Their jewels of silver and jewels of gold?
The prophet of Bethel, we read, told a lie:
He drinks – so did Noah; – he swears – so do I:
To reject him for such peccadillos, were odd;
Besides, he repents – for he talks about G**—   30
                    [*To* Jemmy]
"Never hang down your head, you poor penitent elf,
Come buss me – I'll be Mrs Twitcher myself." '

D–n ye both for a couple of Puritan bitches!
He's Christian enough, that repents, and that stitches.

William Shakespeare to Mrs Anne, Regular Servant to the Revd Mr Precentor of York

A moment's patience, gentle Mistris Anne!
(But stint your clack for sweet St Charitie)
'Tis Willy begs, once a right proper Man,
Tho' now a Book, and interleav'd, you see.
    Much have I born from canker'd Critick's spite,
From fumbling Baronets, and Poets small,
Pert Barristers, & Parsons nothing bright:
But, what awaits me now, is worst of all!
    'Tis true, our Master's temper natural
Was fashion'd fair in meek & dovelike guise: 10
But may not honey's self be turn'd to gall
By residence, by marriage, & sore eyes?
    If then he wreak on me his wicked will:
Steal to his closet at the hour of prayer,
And (when thou hear'st the organ piping shrill)
Grease his best pen, & all he scribbles, tear.
    Better to bottom tarts & cheesecakes nice,
Better the roast-meat from the fire to save,
Better be twisted into caps for spice,
Than thus be patch'd, & cobbled in one's grave!   20
    So York shall taste, what Clouët never knew;
So from *our* works sublimer fumes shall rise:
While Nancy earns the praise to Shakespear due
For glorious puddings, & immortal pies.

On Lord Holland's Seat near Margate, Kent

Old and abandon'd by each venel friend
   Here H[olland] took the pious resolution
To smuggle some few years and strive to mend
   A broken character and constitution.
On this congenial spot he fix'd his choice,
   Earl Godwin trembled for his neighbouring sand,
Here Seagulls scream and cormorants rejoice,
   And Mariners tho' shipwreckt dread to land,
Here reign the blustring north and blighting east,
   No tree is heard to whisper, bird to sing,   10
Yet nature cannot furnish out the feast,
   Art he invokes new horrors still to bring;
Now mouldring fanes and battlements arise,
   Arches and turrets nodding to their fall,
Unpeopled palaces delude his eycs,
   And mimick desolation covers all.
Ah, said the sighing Peer, had Bute been true
   Nor Shelburn's, Rigby's, Calcraft's friendship vain,
Far other scenes than these had bless'd our view
   And realis'd the ruins that we feign.   20
Purg'd by the sword and beautifyed by fire,
   Then had we seen proud London's hated walls,
Owls might have hooted in St Peters Quire,
   And foxes stunk and litter'd in St Pauls.

Ode For Music

I. AIR

'Hence, avaunt ('tis holy ground),
    Comus, and his midnight-crew,
And Ignorance with looks profound,
    And dreaming Sloth of pallid hue,
Mad Sedition's cry profane,
Servitude that hugs her chain,
Nor in these consecrated bowers,
Let painted Flatt'ry hide her serpent-train in flowers.

CHORUS

'Nor Envy base, nor creeping Gain,
Dare the Muse's walk to stain,   10
While bright-eyed Science watches round:
Hence, away, 'tis holy ground!'

II. RECITATIVE

From yonder realms of empyrean day
    Bursts on my ear th' indignant lay:
There sit the sainted sage, the bard divine,
    The few, whom genius gave to shine
Thro' every unborn age, and undiscover'd clime.
    Rapt in celestial transport they:
    Yet hither oft a glance from high
    They send of tender sympathy   20
To bless the place, where on their opening soul
    First the genuine ardour stole.
'Twas Milton struck the deep-ton'd shell,
And, as the choral warblings round him swell,
Meek Newton's self bends from his state sublime
And nods his hoary head, and listens to the rhyme.

III. AIR

    'Ye brown o'er-arching groves,
      That contemplation loves,
Where willowy Camus lingers with delight!
      Oft at the blush of dawn   30

I trod your level lawn,
Oft woo'd the gleam of Cynthia silver-bright
In cloisters dim, far from the haunts of Folly,
With Freedom by my side, and soft-eyed Melancholy.'

IV. RECITATIVE

But hark! the portals sound, and pacing forth
    With solemn steps and slow,
High potentates, and dames of royal birth,
And mitred fathers in long order go:
Great Edward, with the lilies on his brow
    From haughty Gallia torn,   40
And sad Chatillon, on her bridal morn
That wept her bleeding Love, and princely Clare,
And Anjou's heroine, and the paler rose,
The rival of her crown and of her woes,
    And either Henry there,
The murder'd saint, and the majestic lord,
    That broke the bonds of Rome.
(Their tears, their little triumphs o'er,
    Their human passions no more,
Save Charity, that glows beyond the tomb.)   50

ACCOMPANIED

All that on Granta's fruitful plain
Rich streams of regal bounty pour'd,
And bad these awful fanes and turrets rise,
To hail their Fitzroy's festal morning come;
    And thus they speak in soft accord
    The liquid language of the skies:

V. QUARTETTO

'What is grandeur, what is power?
    Heavier toil, superior pain.
    What the bright reward we gain?
    The grateful memory of the good.   60
    Sweet is the breath of vernal shower,
    The bee's collected treasures sweet,
    Sweet music's melting fall, but sweeter yet
    The still small voice of gratitude.'

VI. RECITATIVE

Foremost and leaning from her golden cloud
　　The venerable Marg'ret see!
'Welcome, my noble son (she cries aloud),
　　To this, thy kindred train, and me:
Pleas'd in thy lineaments we trace
A Tudor's fire, a Beaufort's grace.　　　　　　　　　　70

AIR

'Thy liberal heart, thy judging eye,
　　The flow'r unheeded shall descry,
　　And bid it round heav'n's altars shed
　　The fragrance of its blushing head:
　　Shall raise from earth the latent gem
　　To glitter on the diadem.

VII. RECITATIVE

'Lo! Granta waits to lead her blooming band,
　　Not obvious, not obtrusive, she
No vulgar praise, no venal incense flings;
　　Nor dares with courtly tongue refin'd　　　　　　　80
Profane thy inborn royalty of mind:
　　She reveres herself and thee.
With modest pride to grace thy youthful brow,
The laureate wreath, that Cecil wore, she brings,
　　And to thy just, thy gentle hand,
　　Submits the fasces of her sway,
While spirits blest above and men below
Join with glad voice the loud symphonious lay.

VIII. GRAND CHORUS

'Thro' the wild waves as they roar,
　　With watchful eye and dauntless mien,　　　　　　90
　　　Thy steady course of honour keep,
Nor fear the rocks, nor seek the shore:
　　The star of Brunswick smiles serene,
　　　And gilds the horrors of the deep.'

Notes

Abbreviations

Dodsley, *Collection*: *A Collection of Poems . . . By Several Hands*, published by Robert Dodsley, 6 vols (1748–58).

Bentley, *Designs*: *Designs by Mr. R Bentley, for Six Poems by Mr. T. Gray* (1753).

Poems (1768): *Poems by Mr Gray* published by James Dodsley in London and by Andrew and Robert Foulis in Glasgow (1768).

Mason, *Poems*: *The Poems of Mr. Gray, to which are prefixed Memoirs of his Life and Writings* (1775).

Jones, *Poems*: *The Poetical Works of Thomas Gray*, edited by Stephen Jones (1799; 1800).

Gosse, *Poems*: *The Works of Thomas Gray, in Prose and Verse*, ed. Sir Edmund Gosse, 4 vols (1884).

Ode on the Spring Written early in June, 1742, and originally entitled *Noon-tide, An Ode.* First published in Dodsley's *Collection* (vol. ii) in 1748. Gray noted in his Commonplace Book that the poem was written at Stoke Poges and 'sent to Fav. [Richard West] not knowing he was then Dead'. West – only 25 years old – had died of consumption at Hatfield, in Hertfordshire, on 1 June. Gray did not learn of West's death until over two weeks later.

Ode on a Distant Prospect of Eton College Written August 1742, and originally entitled, in Gray's Commonplace Book, *Ode, on a distant Prospect of Windsor, & the adjacent Country.* First published by Robert Dodsley as a folio pamphlet in May, 1747. **Epigraph:** 'I am a man, and that in itself is reason enough for my being miserable.' **l.3 Science:** knowledge, learning. **l.4 Henry's holy shade:** King Henry VI (1422–61), who founded Eton in 1440; Henry's statue still stands in the centre of the Schoolyard at Eton. **l.27 enthral:** imprison. **l.29 rolling circle:** i.e. a hoop trundled by students in play.

Sonnet on the Death of Mr Richard West Written at Stoke Poges in

August 1742, and originally entitled simply *Sonnet*. The poem, which first appeared in Mason's *Poems*, was not published in Gray's lifetime. West had died on 1 June (see note to *Ode on the Spring* above). **l.3 descant:** warbled song.

Ode to Adversity Written at Stoke Poges in August, 1742. First published in Bentley's *Designs* in 1753. **Epigraph:** 'Zeus, who leads mortal men towards understanding, has decreed that wisdom can come only through suffering.' **l.5 adamantine:** made of adamant, unbreakable. **l.7 purple:** purple was the colour often associated with unfettered and arbitrary imperial power. **l.35 Gorgon terrors:** i.e., repulsive aspect, like the gorgons of classical mythology who had snakes for hair.

Hymn to Ignorance Written in the summer of 1742. First published in Mason, *Poems* in 1775. The poem is addressed to Cambridge University. **l.3 Camus:** the river Cam, which flows through Cambridge. **ll.37–8 Sesostris ... harnessed monarchs:** Egyptian conqueror who is said to have yoked his chariot with subjugated kings.

Ode on the Death of a Favourite Cat, Drowned in a Tub of Gold Fishes Written in February 1747. First published in Dodsley, *Collection* in 1748. The piece was composed at Walpole's request as a memorial for his pet cat, Selima, who had drowned after tumbling into a china goldfish bowl at Walpole's London home. **l.3 blow:** bloom, blossom. **l.16 Tyrian hue:** pur ple. **l.34 Nereid:** sea nymph. **l.35 Tom ... Susan:** generic names of household servants. **l.42 Nor all that glisters, gold:** the expression was already proverbial, although Gray appears specifically to be recalling Shakespeare's *Merchant of Venice*, II.vii.65: 'All that glisters is not gold.'

Elegy Written in a Country Churchyard Written primarily between 1746 and June 1750, when a copy of the completed poem was sent to Walpole in London. The beginnings of the *Elegy*, however, may date as far back as 1742. The *Elegy* was first published by Robert Dodsley as a quarto pamphlet in February 1751 (although it had circulated widely in manuscript prior to that date). An earlier draft of the poem – known as the Eton MS and entitled 'Stanzas Wrote in a Country Church-Yard' – remains in the possession of Eton College. **l.16 rude:** untutored, unlearned; specifically, lacking in 'book learning'. **l.26 glebe:** soil. **l.38 trophies:** ornamental memorials. **l.41 storied urn:** an inscribed funeral urn. **l.57 Hampden:** John Hampden (b. 1594) famously championed the rights of Parliament and the people against the 'tyrant' Charles I. He was mortally wounded by Royalists near Oxford in 1643. **l.91 hoary-headed:** grey or white with age. **l.119 science:** knowledge, learning.

A Long Story Written between August and October, 1750. First published in Bentley's *Designs* in March, 1753. Following the circulation in manuscript of the *Elegy* in 1750, Gray came to the attention of his neighbour then living at the Manor House in Stoke Poges, Lady Cobham, her relation, Henrietta Jane Speed, and a friend, Lady Schaub. The poem fancifully recounts an attempt made by the three ladies to visit the poet at West End House, the home of Gray's aunt, Mrs Rogers, and his mother. **ll.2–3 An ancient pile . . . Huntingdons and Hattons:** the manor house at Stoke Poges, built by the Earl of Huntingdon (1535–95), and later said to have been inhabited by Sir Christopher Hatton, Lord Chancellor under Elizabeth I. **l.11 Lord-Keeper:** i.e. Hatton (see note above). **l.25 The first . . . from France:** the first among them, Lady Schaub, came dressed from head to foot in the most fashionable French clothing. **l.35 nom de guerre:** literally 'war name'; the name supposedly given to Lady Cobham when engaged in any fearful enterprise. **l.37 capuchine:** cloak. **l.41 Mr P—t:** Robert Purt, a fellow of King's College, Cambridge. **l.80 a spell:** i.e., a note left for Gray by Lady Schaub informing him of their visit. **l.99 The Lady Janes and Jones:** ghosts haunting the manor house. **1.103 Styack:** the house-keeper. **l.115 Squib:** James Squib, 'Groom of the Chambers', a chaplain long in the service of Lord Cobham. **l.120 Macleane:** James Macleane, a well-known highwayman executed in 1750, who – when called to sentencing – was unable to speak. **l.144 rubbers:** card games.

The Progress of Poesy Written between September, 1751, and December 1754. First published with *The Bard* by Walpole's Strawberry Hill Press in 1757. **Epigraph:** 'Vocal to the intelligent alone.' **l.27 Idalia:** town in Crete where Aphrodite ('Cytherea') was worshipped. **l.68 Ilissus:** stream near Athens. **l.69 Mæander:** famous river in Asia Minor. **l.77 the sad Nine:** the Muses, traditionally associated with Mount Parnassus, near Delphi. **l.78 Latian:** Roman. **l.95 second He:** i.e. John Milton. **l.115 the Theban eagle:** Pindar.

The Bard Written between 1755 and June 1757. First published in with *The Progress of Poesy* 1757. The poem is supposed to be spoken by a Welsh bard who reproaches King Edward I. The King is returning with his army to

England through a deep valley in Snowdonia following his subjugation of
the Welsh in 1283. The bard prophesizes the misfortunes which await the
Plantagenets – 'Edward's race' – while suggesting that nothing will ever
truly subjugate or extinguish the poetic genius indigenous to Britain, a
genius represented by himself. He likewise predicts a poetic revival under
Queen Elizbabeth I and extending into the seventeenth century (foretelling
specifically the achievements of Spenser, Shakespeare and Milton). Having
delivered himself of this prophecy, the bard commits suicide by throwing
himself from the mountain into the river below. **l.1 ruthless King:** Edward I. **l.5 hauberk:** network of steel rings constituting a coat of mail.
l.11 Snowdon: mountainous highlands in north-western Wales.
l.13 Stout Glo'ster: Gilbert de Clare, 8th Earl of Gloucester and King
Edward's son-in-law. **l.14 Mortimer:** Edmond de Mortimer, 6th Baron
Wigmore. **l.16 Conway:** river in northern Wales. **l.28 Hoel's harp**
... Llewellyn's lay: These Welsh names and those which follow –
'Cadwallo', 'Urien', 'Plinlimmon' – refer to the predecessors and 'lost
companions' of the bard. **l.35 Arvon's shore:** the coast of Caernarvon-
shire, opposite the isle of Anglesey. **ll.54–55 When Severn . . . ring:** re-
ferring to the brutal murder of Edward II at Berkeley Castle, in 1327.
l.57 She-wolf of France: Queen Isabel, wife of Edward II, who is
supposed to have had a hand in her husband's murder. **ll.59–60 From**
thee be born ... The scourge of heav'n: Edward III (1327–77).
l.67 the sable warrior: Edward, the Black Prince, who died in 1376.
l.79 he: Richard II (1377–1400). **l.83 the din of battle:** i.e. the Civil
Wars between the Houses of York and Lancaster. **l.87 Ye towers of**
Julius: the Tower of London, begun by William I in the eleventh century.
The oldest part of the Tower was nevertheless supposed by some to have
been built by Julius Caesar. **l.89 his consort's faith:** i.e., the spirit of
Margaret of Anjou, wife of King Henry VI. **l.89 his father's fame:** the
reputation and achievements of King Henry V (1413–22). **l.90 the meek**
usurper: Henry the Sixth (1422–61). **l.93 The bristled boar:** Richard
III (1483–5), who is commonly supposed to have had the uncrowned King
Edward V and his brother Richard killed in the Tower. **l.99 Half of thy**
heart: Eleanor of Castile, wife and queen of Edward I. **l.125 a form**
divine: Elizabeth I. **l.131 great Taliessin:** Taliessin, legendary sixth-
century Welsh bard.

Ode on the Pleasure Arising from Vicissitude Begun in 1754, and never
completed. First published in Mason, *Poems*, in 1775.

Epitaph on Mrs Clerke Written sometime between late 1757 and 31 January 1758. First published in October 1759, in *The Gentleman's Magazine*, and later included in Mason's *Poems* (1775). The epitaph is likewise inscribed on a tablet in St George's Church, Beckenham. Jane Clerke, wife of Gray's acquaintance John Clerke, a physician and fellow of Peterhouse, had died in childbirth in April 1757.

Epitaph on a Child Written in June 1758, and published in Gosse, *Works* (1884). The epitaph was written for Robert (Robin) Wharton – the eldest son of Gray's closest friend, Thomas Wharton – who had died in April, 1758.

The Fatal Sisters Written in 1761, and first published in *Poems* (1768). The poem – along with 'The Descent of Odin' and 'The Triumphs of Owen' – grew out of Gray's plans to write a history of English poetry and is written in the 'Gothic' style. It is taken indirectly from an Icelandic original, the *Darrathar Ljóth*. The circumstances of the encounter retold in the poem, which contains this prophetic account of the Battle of Clontarf are summarised in Gray's Preface to the work. **ll.17–18 Mista ... Sangrida and Hilda:** valkyries, the war maidens of Norse mythology. **l.31 Gondula and Geira:** see note to line 18 above. **l.41 the dauntless earl:** Sigurd. **l.44 a king:** Brian. **l.45 Eirin:** Ireland.

The Descent of Odin Written in 1761 (see note to 'The Fatal Sisters' above), and published in *Poems* (1768). The poem is based upon a Norse original, the *Vegtams Kvitha*. According to Norse mythology, Frigga, the mother of Balder, protected her son from all potentially harmful elements except, inadvertently, mistletoe. The evil spirit and adversary Lok, however, arranged that Balder be struck by a bough of mistletoe held by the blind Hoder. Balder's father Odin, the chief of the Norse gods, undertook a visit to the underworld to learn the fate of his son. The circumstances of this visit are described in Gray's poem. The seer in the underworld names Hoder as Balder's slayer, and further identifies Vali, the son of Odin and Rinda, as the step-brother who will avenge Balder's fate. **l.1 the king of men:** Odin. **l.4 Hela:** the Goddess of Death. **l.5 the dog of darkness:** Gorm, who – like Cerberus in Greek mythology – guards the gates of the underworld. **l.16 portals nine of hell:** the underworld of gothic legend, Niflheimre, was believed to be divided into nine worlds or sections. **l.41 yon glitt'ring board:** presumably the feast prepared for a new arrival in the underworld. **l.75 virgins:** perhaps the Nornir or Fates of Norse mythology.

The Triumphs of Owen: Written in 1760 (see note to 'The Fatal Sisters' above) and published in *Poems* (1768). The poem – a loose translation of a Welsh original – commemorates the victory of Owen, prince of North Wales, over the forces of King Henry II in 1157. **l.3 Roderic:** Roderick, 'prince of Wales', King of Gwynnedd (A.D. 844–78). **l.4 Gwyneth:** in northern Wales. **l.14 Lochlin:** Denmark. **l.15 Norman:** i.e. Norwegian. **l.20 Mona:** the isle of Anglesey. **l.25 Talymalfra:** i.e., Moelfre, a bay on the isle of Anglesey.

Sketch of his Own Character Written in the spring of 1761 and published in Mason, *Poems* in 1775. **l.6 Charles Townshend and Squire:** Charles Townshend (1735–67), recently appointed Secretary of War, and Dr Samuel Squire, a newly-made Bishop.

Song I (' 'Midst beauty and pleasure's gay triumphs to languish'): Written sometime before October, 1761 and first printed (within a footnote) in an edition of the *Works* of Alexander Pope edited by Joseph Warton in 1797. The poem may have been produced by Gray specifically for Miss Henrietta Jane Speed, following her request that she might 'possess something from his pen . . . on the subject of *love*'.

Song II ('Thyrsis, when we parted, swore') Written in October 1761, and first published in the *European Magazine* in February 1791. See note to *Song I* above.

The Candidate Written early in 1764 and first printed that same year. The poem was not published with Gray's other works until Stephen Jones included it in the second edition of his *Poems* (1800). The occasion of Gray's satire was the contest for the high Stewardship of Cambridge in 1764. Candidates for the position included John Montagu, 4th Earl of Sandwich, who had years before been a schoolfellow of Gray's at Eton. Montagu's candidacy was countered by that of Lord Royston, who was promoted by the Duke of Newcastle, who had been elected Chancellor of the University in 1749. **l.1 Jemmy Twitcher:** Lord Sandwich, so-called after the untrustworthy and self-serving character of the same name in John Gay's *The Beggar's Opera*. **l.3 three sisters:** the faculties of Medicine, Jurisprudence, and Divinity at Cambridge. **l.6 sheep-biting:** sneaky. **l.8 his nose is a shame:** due, it is implied, to the ravages of venereal disease. **l.12 Rochester's book:** the works of John Wilmot, 2nd Earl of Rochester, which were considered by many to be lewd and licentious. **l.14 a**

wife: Lady Sandwich went insane and was incarcerated. She in fact lived until 1779. **l.17 Newgate-bird:** criminal. **l.24 catches:** songs. The Old Testament King David was of course thought to have written the Psalms. **l.34 stitches:** i.e. whores; lies with women.

William Shakespeare to Mrs Anne, Regular Servant to the Revd Mr Precentor of York Written in July 1765, and first printed in John Mitford's *Correspondence of Thomas Gray and William Mason* in 1853. The precentor of the poem's title was Gray's close friend William Mason, who had been Canon Residentiary and Precentor of York since 1762. The supposed protestations and concerns expressed by 'Willy' Shakespeare's volume in the poem are occasioned by the fact that Mason was at the time preparing an annotated 'edition' of Shakespeare's plays. **l.21 Clouët:** famous French chef of the Duke of Newcastle.

On Lord Holland's Seat near Margate, Kent Written in June, 1768, and published without Gray's permission the following year. Lord Holland (Henry Fox), former Paymaster General and Leader of the House of Commons, had begun constructing his odd and fanciful residence, replete with mock ruins and follies, at Kingsgate, near Margate, in 1763. Gray, who had – thanks largely to the information he received through Walpole – followed Fox's political career closely, was not alone in his assessment of the former minister as a deceitful and untrustworthy time-server. **l.6 Earl Godwin:** i.e. the Goodwin sands off the Kentish coast, traditionally the remains of an island belonging to the medieval Earl of Goodwine. **l.17 Bute:** the Earl of Bute, the Prime Minister and Holland's former patron. **l.18 Shelburn's . . . Rigby's . . . Calcraft's friendship:** former political allies mentioned by name in one of Holland's own poems, *Lord Holland returning from Italy* (1767).

Ode for Music Written between February and April, 1769. The *Ode* celebrated the formal installation of the Duke of Grafton as Chancellor of Cambridge University. Gray's work was set to music by John Randall, Professor of Music at Cambridge, and performed at the festivities marking the Installation at the Senate House on 1 July 1769. The *Ode* was published by the University printer (in two editions) that same year. **l.2 Comus:** mythical tempter and pagan god, the son of Circe and Bacchus who featured in John Milton's masque of the same name. **l.11 Science:** learning. **l.21 the place:** i.e., Cambridge. **l.29 Camus:** the river Cam.

l.39 Great Edward: King Edward III (1312–77). **l.40 haughty Gallia:**
France; King Edward had added the 'lilies' or fleur de lys of France to the
arms of England. **l.41 sad Chatillon:** Marie de Valentia, Countess of
Pembroke and founder of Pembroke College (1343). Her husband was said
to have been slain on their wedding day. **l.42 princely Clare:** Elizabeth
de Burg, Countess of Clare and founder of Clare Hall (1342). **l.43 Anjou's
heroine:** Margaret of Anjou, founder of Queens' College (1448).
l.43 the paler rose: Elizabeth Widville, wife of Edward IV; she continued
the work of Margaret of Anjou, and granted Queens' College its statutes.
l.45 either Henry: Henry VI ('the murthered saint') and Henry VIII
('the majestic lord'). Henry VI founded King's College (1441) and Henry
VIII in 1546 united two existing colleges to create Trinity College.
l.54 Fitzroy: i.e. the Duke of Grafton, born Augustus Henry Fitzroy.
l.66 The venerable Marg'ret: Countess of Richmond and Derby. She
founded both St John's College (1508) and Christ's College (1505).
l.70 Tudor ... Beaufort: Grafton traced his descent through both
families. **l.84 Cecil:** William Cecil, Lord Treasurer Burleigh, Chancellor
of the University under Queen Elizabeth I. **l.86 fasces:** symbolic rods
indicating institutional authority. **l.93 The star of Brunswick:** i.e.
King George III and, by extension, the House of Brunswick in general.

Everyman's Poetry

Titles available in this series **all at £1.00**

William Blake
ed. Peter Butter
0 460 87800 X

Robert Burns
ed. Donald Low
0 460 87814 X

Samuel Taylor Coleridge
ed. John Beer
0 460 87826 3

Thomas Gray
ed. Robert Mack
0 460 87805 0

Ivor Gurney
ed. George Walter
0 460 87797 6

George Herbert
ed. D. J. Enright
0 460 87795 X

Robert Herrick
ed. Douglas Brooks-Davies
0 460 87799 2

John Keats
ed. Nicholas Roe
0 460 87808 5

**Henry Wadsworth
Longfellow**
ed. Anthony Thwaite
0 460 87821 2

John Milton
ed. Gordon Campbell
0 460 87813 1

Edgar Allan Poe
ed. Richard Gray
0 460 87804 2

Poetry Please!
Foreword by Charles
Causley
0 460 87824 7

Alexander Pope
ed. Douglas Brooks-Davies
0 460 87798 4

Lord Rochester
ed. Paddy Lyons
0 460 87819 0

Christina Rossetti
ed. Jan Marsh
0 460 87820 4

William Shakespeare
ed. Martin Dodsworth
0 460 87815 8

Alfred, Lord Tennyson
ed. Michael Baron
0 460 87802 6

R. S. Thomas
ed. Anthony Thwaite
0 460 87811 5

Walt Whitman
ed. Ellman Crasnow
0 460 87825 5

Oscar Wilde
ed. Robert Mighall
0 460 87803 4